A STUDY OF THE
BOOK OF GENESIS

Fresh
START

Written by Rachel Booth Smith | Designed by Morgan Broom
Copyright © 2025 by Proverbs 31 Ministries
All Scripture quotations are English Standard Version (ESV) unless otherwise noted.

WE MUST EXCHANGE *whispers* WITH GOD BEFORE *shouts* WITH THE WORLD.

LYSA TERKEURST

PAIR YOUR STUDY GUIDE WITH THE FIRST 5 MOBILE APP!

This study guide is designed to accompany your study of Scripture in the First 5 mobile app. You can use it as a standalone study or as an accompanying guide to the daily content within First 5. First 5 is a free mobile app developed by Proverbs 31 Ministries to transform your daily time with God.

Go to the app store on your smartphone, download the First 5 app, and create a free account!

WWW.FIRST5.ORG

WELCOME

Every writer stares at a blank page and feels the pressure of their first line. In *A Tale of Two Cities*, Charles Dickens wrote, "It was the best of times, it was the worst of times …" pulling us in as we wonder how it could be both. Even the *Star Wars* opening — "A long time ago, in a galaxy far, far away" — grabs the audience as we settle in for a great movie.

The first sentence of a story hopefully snatches the readers' hearts and minds and inspires them to read on.

In Hebrew, the opening phrase of Genesis is one word: *B'reshith*, (pronounced "buh-rey-SHEET"). In the Jewish literary tradition, some book titles are taken from the first words of the book, and Genesis is titled "In the Beginning" in Hebrew, with the understanding that this book is all about beginnings.

"In the beginning, God created the heavens and the earth" (Genesis 1:1).

For all the stories ever told and books ever written, nothing compares to this epic opening. The first line tugs the reader out of our setting and transports our minds farther into the past than we've ever explored. Genesis takes us to the beginning of time — and the beginning of the gospel, the greatest story ever.

We can see God's good story in Scripture almost like a five-act play:

1. **Creation.**
2. **Fall.**
3. **Israel.**
4. **Jesus.**
5. **Church.**

The story is told across 66 books of the Bible, with God as the main character. Scripture starts with God's delight in the good world He **created**, then tells of humankind's rebellion against God **(the fall)**. Genesis gives us these first two acts, and it also lays the foundation for the third act, where the story takes an upward turn with God's restoration of His people in and through **Israel**. But humanity still needed a Savior — so the whole story culminates in the life, death, resurrection and ascension of **Jesus**, an Israelite man who is also the Son of God. And now God has sent His Spirit to work through **the Church** (believers in Jesus) to continue His restoration plan.

to GENESIS

As we begin our study, Genesis bids us to sit down at the beginning of the play and watch this story unfold. We can observe as the audience, taking in the choices of the characters and watching God act gently with firm grace. The invitation, though, is to watch from backstage. For believers in Jesus, this is our story. In this five-act play, *we are participants in the final act*. We step on stage and enter the story, interacting with the God who has proven His faithfulness.

Friend, this invitation is open to you. Even if you've only ever watched God's story from the audience. Even if you've only seen Act 4 or glimpsed Act 2. Even if you're feeling hopeless and desperate because of past mistakes that seem to pile up, leaving you gasping for air and unable to see your way out. Even if you're wondering whether God is who He claims to be or you're sad about the state of the world.

If so, you'll find lots of company in Genesis. Here we will see what God wanted the world to look like and how He restores things when we can't see a way out. Here we will set down our failures and let God teach us who He is. And as we get to know Him, whether for the first time or once again, here we will learn He is good and trustworthy.

Let's start fresh together. From the beginning, we can see God's story play out from the wings of the theater, enthralled by the action and thrilled we get a chance to enter in.

Join me backstage, friends. This is your story too.

WARMLY,

Major THEMES

THEME NO. 1: **GOD'S IDENTITY AND OUR IDENTITY**

It's hard to view life outside of our own circumstances, and sometimes negative events seem to overwhelm the positive. Our experiences with struggles like mental health, financial strain, relationship challenges, illness, injustice and loss have fractured life's lens. Our perspective is skewed.

But Genesis gives us a way to hold truths in tension by adding an "and." Life is hard, *and* God is good, *and* He made us for a good purpose. This book invites us to recalibrate our view of life as we know it and to see life as God designed it.

Genesis theologically teaches *who God is* and *who we are*. To answer the question "who is God?" the stories in Genesis showcase His character of righteousness, mercy and faithfulness. These same stories answer the question "who are we?" as they highlight the delight God has in us, the blessings He longs to bestow on us, and the purpose He has for us. At the same time, Genesis also doesn't shy away from showing how our choices have consequences and how we and our communities experience the brokenness of sin.

Genesis 1 describes God's perfect order, but the story quickly descends into terrible disorder because of human rebellion against God (sin). Thankfully, God had — and still has — a restoration plan. Throughout Genesis, we can learn about God's character and ours, His plans and ours, His faithfulness and our brokenness. The miracle in Genesis is that despite the disparity between us and God, He still reached down repeatedly to let people in on His plan for redemption and even blessed them along the way. Our false starts and broken stories have never deterred God; nothing can stop His good plans.

THEME NO. 2: **BLESSINGS AND CURSES**

✦ BLESSINGS AND CURSES FROM GOD

Blessings are benefits God freely gives to those He favors.[1] In the time of Genesis, God's gifts to His people were often related to fertility, land, food and security, serving as a powerful relationship builder and indicator of His love.[2] God's intent and desire is to bless. *He loves us.*

But in contrast to blessings, curses in Genesis were consequences for people choosing anything outsideof God's good boundaries. Curses resulted in death, alienation and hostility — the opposite of abundant life.[3]

God's plans and parameters for us are designed to keep the good things in and the bad things out! Throughout Genesis, God upheld His creation by both His blessings and His curses.[4]

✦ PATRIARCHAL BLESSINGS

Genesis shows us a God who loves to bless His people, and in these scriptures, we also see familial blessings passed down by the people themselves. In the Ancient Near East (the cultural and historical setting of Genesis), fathers gave blessings to their children as a way of prayerfully sharing their hopes and wishes for those children.[5] Such blessings often invoked God's name but were not necessarily predictive of the children's future. As one scholar puts it, "Man is never able to coerce God into blessing him, nor is man able to acquire blessing from a source besides God."[6]

✦ BIRTHRIGHT

Related to the idea of patriarchal blessings is the concept of a "birthright," which was traditionally given to the oldest son in an Ancient Near Eastern family. The birthright included a double portion of the family's material wealth, along with the foremost blessing from the father who was the head of the family (the patriarch). The oldest son was legally entitled to the birthright (Deuteronomy 21:17).

✦ COVENANT BLESSING OF ISRAEL

God established a covenant — a relationship founded on His character and promises — with a man named Abram in Genesis 12:1-3. This covenant passed from Abram to his son Isaac, then from Isaac to his son Jacob, then from Jacob to his 12 sons, who became the nation of Israel. The covenant blessing was given from father to son but was confirmed and carried out by God Himself.

THEME NO. 3: **COVENANT**

In its simplest form, covenants are binding agreements that define a relationship between the parties involved. One example of a biblical covenant is marriage: It defines the partnership between husband and wife and is intended to last for a lifetime. In Genesis, there are human covenants between one person and another (e.g., Genesis 21:27-32; Genesis 26:26-31; Genesis 31:44-54) as well as divine covenants between God and people (e.g., Genesis 9:11; Genesis 15:18; Genesis 17:21). These covenants always included an oath and often included food — "a meal and a deal." Divine covenants tell us about God's expectations for us in relationship to Him and about God's faithfulness in relationship to us.

How IS GENESIS STRUCTURED?

Genesis is an intricate and well-crafted book. If you were to open a table of contents for this book in its original language, the chapter headings would all start with the Hebrew word *toledot*. In English, this word is often translated as "the generations," a phrase that helps us distinguish different eras in the history of God's people.

The first part of Genesis (Chapters 1-11) covers five distinct eras and depicts the history of the world's origins. The second part of Genesis (Chapters 12-50) follows the story of Abram's descendants throughout five additional eras.

PART ONE: **GENESIS 1-11**

Genesis 1-11 describes the beginnings of the world and is similar in style and content to some other stories from across the Ancient Near East (ANE). Other ANE stories included creation accounts, like we see in Genesis 1-2, and they often had a flood account, like we see in Genesis 6-9. But while other ANE stories explained reality with reference to myths and false gods, we know Genesis tells the *true story* of creation with the *true God* at the center. Genesis does not "borrow" from other mythologies, but God did choose to communicate His Truth using a style the original culture could readily understand, which sometimes means the stories in Scripture have similarities to other narratives.

Within the Genesis account, God revealed beautiful attributes of His character in an accessible way, yet He also contrasted Himself with ANE cultural and religious norms centered on pagan deities. The first section of Genesis, the story of the world's origins, paints a vivid picture of God's constant character and humanity's inconstancy. We get peeks at God's delight in His creation, especially His delight in humanity, and at what He considers good and orderly for our thriving (Genesis 1:31). We also catch glimpses of His long patience and how He addressed the darkness that threatened to overcome us and our world: When things got rough, God purposefully and calmly reestablished order (Genesis 3:22-24; Genesis 6:5-8).

PART TWO: **GENESIS 12-50**

The second section of Genesis, the story of Israel, starts with one man named Abram (also called Abraham) and God's stated purpose to bless the entire world through him (Genesis 12:1-3). Throughout the stories of Abram's family, we'll see a lot of brokenness, but God gently corrected His people and reestablished order, all while moving the storyline toward His promised blessing for all peoples through one family.

In terms of style, Genesis 12-50 often uses the literary form of historical narrative. These true stories of Israel's patriarchs are not exhaustive biographies recounting everything they experienced; they give us the most important details and leave others out. Just as you or I might tell a true story about something that happened at the grocery store and shape it to get our point across, so do the authors of biblical accounts. In telling our story, we may not mention the sale on apples, but we might highlight the cashier's kindness. Similarly, the stories in Genesis are certainly designed to share facts, but knowing that these stories are also told with an end goal in mind can help us be good readers.

The goal of all Scripture is to testify about God's redemptive plan (John 5:39), and Genesis gives us a view into how that plan has been taking shape since the beginning. Perhaps most importantly, Genesis introduces us not only to what our God is doing but to *who our God is* and how He's so very good.

GENESIS
TABLE *of* CONTENTS

PART ONE

HISTORY OF THE WORLD'S ORIGINS (IN FIVE ERAS)

01 — Generations of the Heavens and Earth

"These are the generations of the heavens and the earth when they were created ..." (Genesis 2:4).

02 — Generations of Adam

"This is the book of the generations of Adam ..." (Genesis 5:1).

03 — Generations of Noah

"These are the generations of Noah ..." (Genesis 6:9).

04 — Generations of Shem, Ham and Japheth

"These are the generations of the sons of Noah, Shem, Ham, and Japheth ..." (Genesis 10:1).

"These are the clans of the sons of Noah ..." (Genesis 10:32).

05 — Generations of Shem

"These are the generations of Shem ..." (Genesis 11:10).

PART TWO

HISTORY OF ISRAEL (IN FIVE MORE ERAS)

06 — Generations of Terah (tells the story of Abraham)

"Now these are the generations of Terah. Terah fathered Abram ..." (Genesis 11:27).

07 — Generations of Ishmael

"These are the generations of Ishmael, Abraham's son ..." (Genesis 25:12).

08 — Generations of Isaac (tells the story of Jacob)

"These are the generations of Isaac, Abraham's son ..." (Genesis 25:19).

09 — Generations of Esau

"These are the generations of Esau (that is, Edom)" (Genesis 36:1).

"These are the generations of Esau the father of the Edomites ..." (Genesis 36:9).

10 — Generations of Jacob (tells the story of Joseph and his brothers)

"These are the generations of Jacob ..." (Genesis 37:2).

Main CHARACTERS IN THE BOOK OF *Genesis*

ADAM AND **EVE**

The first man and woman were made by God in His image, designed to be His representatives in His creation, according to Genesis 1:27-28. God gave them tasks and work in the garden of Eden, where they had a relationship with each other and with God that was marked by completely unashamed vulnerability (Genesis 2:25). But they fell into the temptation to be the determiners of good and evil, to become "*like God*" (Genesis 3:5). After they rebelled against God, their relationships with each other and with God were marked by shame and hiding (Genesis 3:7-8), and they were exiled from the garden (Genesis 3:23-24).

NOAH

Noah was a man whose life pleased God during a time when *"the wickedness of man was great in the earth, and ... every intention of the thoughts of his heart was only evil continually"* (Genesis 6:5). God called Noah to build an ark (a very large boat) for himself, his family and many animals. This ark saved them from an overwhelming flood God brought on the earth. After the flood, God gave the same instructions to Noah and his family that He had given to Adam and Eve (Genesis 8:15-17). Order was reestablished, and creation started over.

THE **PATRIARCHS** OF **ISRAEL**

The word "patriarch" comes from two Greek words: *patria* (meaning "family") and *arkhes* (meaning "beginning" or "ruler"). Specifically, a "patriarch" is the male leader of a family. The three patriarchs associated with the family of Israel are Abraham, Isaac and Jacob; God established a covenant with them.

- ABRAM (ALSO CALLED ABRAHAM).
  Abram started as a worshipper of foreign gods from Ur but then received God's abundant promises and obeyed God. His story had ups and downs but was marked by his faith that God was who He said He was and would do what He promised.

  Abraham was married to Sarai (also called Sarah). She was barren, but God miraculously enabled her to have a son, Isaac, because she considered God faithful (Hebrews 11:11). Before Isaac was born, Abraham had a son named Ishmael with Sarai's servant Hagar. But it was Isaac, not Ishmael, who continued the covenant with God.

- ISAAC.
  He was Abraham's son, the fulfillment of God's promise. Isaac married Rebekah, and they had twins: Esau and Jacob. The covenant passed from Isaac to Jacob.

- JACOB (ALSO CALLED ISRAEL).
  He was Isaac's son, and his life was troubled by his trickster nature and tendency to manipulate situations to achieve his desired outcome. Nevertheless, God was faithful to extend His covenant through Jacob. God renamed him "Israel" in Genesis 32:28 after he wrestled with God.

  Jacob married sisters named Leah and Rachel and had children with them. He also had children with their maids, Zilpah and Bilhah. The descendants of Jacob's 12 sons eventually became the 12 tribes of the nation of Israel.

  One of Jacob's sons, **Joseph**, was sold into slavery in Egypt. Joseph's unexpected story of rising to power in Egypt makes up 12 chapters at the end of Genesis.

  Also noteworthy is Jacob's oldest son, **Judah**, who had children with his own daughter-in-law, Tamar (Genesis 38). In His human lineage, Jesus Himself is a descendant of Judah (Matthew 1:1-16)! Across generations, God always had a plan for redemption through this family tree.

THE CONTEXT of GENESIS

GEOGRAPHICAL SETTING

While the geographical setting of Genesis 1-11 is not specified in Scripture, Genesis 12-50 takes place across a region now known as the Fertile Crescent. The history of Israel started with Abraham's early life in Ur (modern-day Iraq); then he moved to Haran (modern-day Turkey), down into Canaan (modern-day Israel and Palestine), and all the way to Egypt. After Abraham's death (Genesis 25:8), the rest of the Genesis story takes place largely in Canaan and Egypt.

During this time, there weren't established countries with borders like we might think of today. Rather, there were walled cities with leaders controlling and competing for the regions around their cities. For instance, the city-state of Babylon had a relatively large city and controlled the territory around that city. These regions regularly changed in size and leadership.

CULTURAL SETTING

Abraham, Isaac and Jacob lived within the cultural context of the Ancient Near East (ANE). The descendants of these patriarchs would eventually become the nation of Israel, but in Genesis, they were still part of the larger ANE culture. This is similar to the way people from a U.S. state — Tennessee, for instance — are culturally distinct from other U.S. citizens in some ways, but they are also part of a larger U.S., Western culture.

Before the book of Genesis was formally written, many of its truths may have been passed down orally. Still, people first encountered the written form of Genesis in the ANE, and they would have seen how Genesis both adopted and tweaked some of their existing cultural concepts (for instance, covenant or circumcision). Genesis also makes theological statements that would have been new and astounding to the surrounding culture (for instance, God created a garden to inhabit *with humanity* in Genesis 1, which was virtually unheard of in pagan mythologies). In any case, having a grasp of some ancient cultural norms can help us understand the truths God was communicating.

For example, it's interesting to note that many ANE languages had a common foundation (which is why modern linguists group them together as "Semitic" languages). Although different city-states spoke different dialects, much of their vocabulary was similar. For instance, the Babylonian word for "sun" was *shamash*, and the Hebrew word for "sun" is *shemesh*. ANE city-states also had their own law codes, though across different regions there were similar standards with varying emphases. Finally, each city-state could have its own religious pantheon (many gods the people would worship locally), with different gods on the top tier.

Besides people who lived in cities, there were also wide-ranging tribal groups who lived in settlements mostly outside of cities. In fact, Abraham's family may have started out either in the city of Ur or in the settlements around the city (Genesis 11:31; Genesis 15:7). Abraham was a nomadic shepherd who migrated with his family and livestock. Sometimes they stopped outside of towns; sometimes they set up their own camps. Their travel schedule was dictated by factors like seasons or famine.

Picturing Abraham traveling as a shepherd with a large group of people and animals he was responsible for can change how we read Genesis. As we read, let's try to imagine the sights, smells, sounds and people Abraham and his family interacted with. Of course, as modern people, we can't fully grasp every aspect of ANE culture, but even a small glimpse can help us step out of our sneakers and into their sandals.

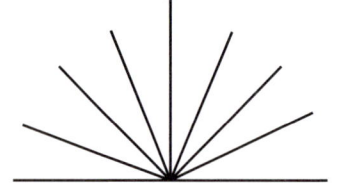

AUTHOR & LITERARY FEATURES *of* GENESIS

AUTHOR OF GENESIS

Genesis is the first book in the Bible and is also the first book in a five-part series within Scripture called the Pentateuch. This series consists of Genesis, Exodus, Leviticus, Numbers and Deuteronomy. These five books are also sometimes referenced as the Law or the Torah.

The Israelite leader Moses had a prominent hand in the writing of the Pentateuch, as we can see from various Bible passages (Exodus 17:14; Numbers 33:2; Joshua 1:7-8; Nehemiah 13:1). Jesus Himself also seemed to treat Moses as the author of the Law when He referenced what *"Moses said"* in the Ten Commandments (Mark 7:10), which was inseparable from the entire Pentateuch.

Still, a singular author of the book of Genesis is not specifically mentioned in Scripture. Many scholars attribute the authorship to several sources or suggest several editors may have added material.[1] One thing we know for sure is that the book of Genesis you and I hold in our hands has not been changed or altered in any significant way since its presentation in the finalized canon of Scripture (the collection of writings officially accepted as God's true and perfect Word). The canon "does not deny that there are a variety of human authors, styles, and messages, but the final authority [of Scripture] is grounded in origin with God himself."[2]

LITERARY FEATURES OF GENESIS

Ancient Hebrew narratives (like Genesis) were distinct from those of other cultures in a few ways. Literary techniques like repetition and chiasm, for instance, would not have surprised an Israelite; the readers or listeners would have recognized what the author was signaling to them. Much of what was written in the Old Testament was first passed down verbally from memory, so these writing styles also came from and promote memorization. Since some of these styles are not typical today, we might miss them altogether or wonder why the author was repeating himself. Let's learn a bit more so we know what to look for!

SYMMETRY, BALANCE AND REPETITION

Symmetry, balance and repetition often highlight important events and truths in the Old Testament.[3] For instance, Genesis 1 repeats versions of the phrase *"and God saw that it was good"* **seven times** (vv. 4, 10, 12, 18, 21, 25, 31). The author wants the reader to walk away from this chapter thinking, *God makes good things. He must be a good God.*

We see another example of repetition in Genesis as God repeated the Abrahamic covenant promise (Genesis 12:1-3; Genesis 17:4-6; Genesis 18:18; Genesis 22:17-18; etc.). There are slight variations in some of these repetitions — not to suggest that God forgot what He'd said previously but to draw the reader to watch which aspects of His promise stayed exactly the same and which were broadened. By repeating the promise, God ensured that His faithfulness, rather than human failures, remained the focus.

CHIASM

Chiasm is a way of structuring a piece of writing to highlight the information at the center or in the middle. A chiasm is formed when a sentence, section, chapter or book leads up to an event or conclusion (the important midpoint), then repeats itself in reverse. For example, take a look at Matthew 6:24, where Jesus used a chiasm in the Sermon on the Mount:

> "No one can serve two masters,
>   for either he will hate the one
>   and love the other,
>   or he will be devoted to the one
>   and despise the other.
> You cannot serve God and money."

Chiasms are a testimony to the artistry of the biblical authors, and they also give us insight into the main idea the author is trying to show us.[4] The entire story of Noah is a famous chiasm in Genesis: The key middle scripture is Genesis 8:1, which is about God's remembrance of Noah.[5] (You can read more about this chiasm on Page 48!)

Hopefully these notes about authorship, writing style and context have helped us lay the groundwork for our study of this amazing book in God's Word. Now that we have a foundation to build on ... *let's get started!*

MAJOR

WEEK ONE

GENESIS 1–2:3
God created the world and all that is in it.

GENESIS 2:4-25
Creation was described again, detailing humanity's purpose.

GENESIS 3:1-13
Humans disobeyed and undermined God's order.

GENESIS 3:14-21
God cursed the serpent and the ground and gave consequences to humanity.

GENESIS 3:22-24
Adam and Eve were forced to leave Eden, exiled because of their disobedience.

WEEK TWO

GENESIS 4:1-16
Cain and Abel revealed the consequences of envy and murder.

GENESIS 4:17–5:32
A lineage from Adam to Noah marked the passing of many generations.

GENESIS 6–9
God saved Noah and his family from the waters of the great flood.

GENESIS 10–11:26
The tower of Babel incident resulted in the scattering of humanity.

GENESIS 11:27–12:9
God called Abram.

MOMENTS

WEEK THREE

GENESIS 12:10-20
Abram and his family traveled to Egypt during a famine.

GENESIS 13-14
Abram and Lot parted ways.

GENESIS 15
God established a covenant with Abram.

GENESIS 16
God saw and heard Hagar.

GENESIS 17
God's covenant was solidified with Abram, now called Abraham.

WEEK FOUR

GENESIS 18-19
The sinful cities of Sodom and Gomorrah faced divine judgment.

GENESIS 20
Abraham navigated challenges with Abimelech.

GENESIS 21
Isaac was born, and Hagar and Ishmael were sent away.

GENESIS 22
Abraham was tested.

GENESIS 23-24
Rebekah's story unfolded.

WEEK **FIVE**

GENESIS 25–26:33
Jacob and Esau would become two nations, and Esau sold his birthright.

GENESIS 26:34–28:9
Jacob stole Esau's blessing.

GENESIS 28:10-22
God restated to Jacob the covenant He had started with Abram.

GENESIS 29–30
Jacob married Laban's daughters and had children, and his flocks increased.

GENESIS 31
Jacob ran from Laban.

WEEK **SIX**

GENESIS 32–33
Jacob met with Esau and wrestled with God.

GENESIS 34
Dinah was assaulted, and her brothers retaliated brutally.

GENESIS 35–36
Jacob followed through on his promise to God at El-bethel.

GENESIS 37
Joseph's story began with his dreams and coat of many colors.

GENESIS 38
Judah was concerned for his property and land, and his family line continued through Tamar.

WEEK **SEVEN**

GENESIS 39
Joseph faced challenges in Potiphar's house.

GENESIS 40-41
Joseph interpreted dreams and had a dramatic rise to power in Egypt.

GENESIS 42-45
Joseph's brothers traveled to Egypt, unaware of Joseph's true identity, leading to a pivotal reunion.

GENESIS 46-47:26
Jacob's family moved to Egypt.

GENESIS 47:27-50:26
Jacob blessed his sons.

WEEK
One

Day 1 - GENESIS **1-2:3**

God created the world and all that is in it.

Welcome to a study of beginnings — the beginning of the world, the beginning of sin, and the beginning of God's redemption plan. As we spend time in God's Word, may we encounter God's goodness in Genesis and grow a deeper trust in His character.

This first chapter, with its brief and clean descriptions, gives us insight into who God is. And He is pretty remarkable. The world was not an afterthought or slapdash project of His — it was perfectly designed by a good God who makes good things.

Scholars have noted that Scripture describes God's creation of **habitats** during the first three days of creation, and during the next three days, He filled the habitats with **inhabitants**.[1]

- Spend some time reading Genesis 1-2:3, and fill in the chart below. (We've provided a few answers for you.)

HABITAT	INHABITANTS
DAY ONE THE HABITAT OF **TIME** God created: Day and Night	DAY FOUR INHABITING THE **HEAVENS** God created: _____
DAY TWO THE HABITAT OF **CLIMATE** God created: _____	DAY FIVE INHABITING THE **SEAS AND SKIES** God created: Fish and Birds
DAY THREE THE HABITAT OF **AGRICULTURE** God created: _____	DAY SIX INHABITING THE **LAND** God created: _____
DAY SEVEN God rested.	

For six days, God created a sacred and lovely space, pronouncing blessings and putting things in a perfect order. On the seventh day, God rested. To the Ancient Near Eastern (ANE) person, this meant God took a seat on His throne. His job of creating was complete, everything was just right, and He sat to reign over it. The word "*rested*" in Genesis 2:2 is an active, engaged term: God wasn't acting like an earthly father who might passively nap while the kids run around. He was ruling His Kingdom, continuing to sustain all of creation.
- Have you ever thought about God's **rest** as God's **reign**? How might this perspective change your understanding of the seventh day of the creation account?

Perhaps the biggest theological statement made by Genesis 1-2:3 is that the world we experience today is not the unbroken world God originally intended for us. His good and ordered plan is laid out in these scriptures. Our broken relationships, broken work and broken homes were not in the design. The realities of disease, thorns and disharmony were not in the design. So today when we point out our wounds to God, He doesn't tell us to get over them. He agrees that they're wounds — that the world is broken.

The natural question, then, is: Why do we experience the world as broken if that's not how God designed it? Hold on to that thought. We will come to the answer in Genesis 3.

For now, let's read Genesis 2:1-3 and compare the seventh day to the other six days of creation. In the introduction to this study, we mentioned the importance of repetition in Hebrew writings, and you may have noticed how the statement *"there was evening and there was morning"* signals the end of each day of creation in Genesis 1:5-31.
- Does the seventh day (described in Genesis 2:1-3) have an end like the other six days? What might this mean about God's reign?

In a sense, the seventh day persists, even though the good order God put together for our world differs from what we see today. As one scholar observes, "He remains enthroned—patient, holy, merciful, trustworthy, and powerful—drawing us back to His purposes with kindness (Romans 2:4). When our hearts are aching, searching for a reprieve from our problems or a place to grieve our loss, day seven says: *Rest here at the throne.*"[2]

THE IMAGE of GOD

In Genesis, God distinguished Himself from ancient cultural norms. One way He did this was by declaring in Genesis 1:26a, *"Let us make man in our image, after our likeness."* As modern readers, many of us may understand we are made in the image of God and continue reading without further consideration. People across the ANE, however, understood the image of God in two contexts:

First, sometimes "image of god" referred to an image or icon of a false god set in a temple, acting as a representative of that god. This practice is idolatry, which God prohibits in the Ten Commandments in Exodus 20. The word we translate from Hebrew into English as "idol" can also be translated as *"carved image"* (Exodus 20:4).

Second, the phrase "image of god" was also used by ANE cultures to refer to kings because many people believed the gods ruled the world through their appointed kings. Kings, as "images of god" or divine representatives, would govern and lead on behalf of their gods. The kings supposedly imparted the values and precepts that were important to the gods.[1]

When the one true God used this well-known idea from the ancient world to describe man and woman in Genesis 1, this was an astounding decree! He stated that *all of humankind* is created to reflect Him and His principles to the world.

We carry this _identity_ with us as we do the **tasks** He has assigned us.

1. We are to *"be fruitful and multiply"* (Genesis 1:28), _reproducing God's image_ in the world. This can include raising children but can also include other fruitful labor and disciple-making in God's Kingdom, often requiring harmony and partnership with our fellow image bearers.

2. We are to *"fill the earth and subdue it"* (Genesis 1:28) as *God's image bearers*, not as violent authoritarians with our own agenda but as those who care for the earth as His creation.

3. We are to *"have dominion"* (Genesis 1:28) as *God's image bearers*, reflecting His creativity and order, using justice and mercy.

In the ANE, the average man was a land worker. He believed his role in life was to ease the burden of the gods by working the land and considered this a privilege. He also sent his produce to the so-called "image of god," the king, to provide sustenance for the gods.

When God declared that all men and women are made in His image, in essence He declared that "kingship has been democratized. Not just kings but all humans bear this royal badge of divinity."[2]

And did you catch that both *men and women* are made in God's image? In contrast to many other ancient creation accounts, Genesis specifically includes both genders. Men and women, both individually and working together in community, act as God's image bearers.

God has given humans identity, responsibilities and honor, letting us reflect Him to His good creation. This kingship democratization is astounding. God says *every person and their work,* from the farmer to the potter to the seamstress, is as valuable, purposeful and sacred as a king. This is still true today of the teacher, the executive, the janitor, the stay-at-home mom, the insurance salesman — and you and me.[3]

Day 2 - GENESIS **2:4-25**

Creation was described again, detailing humanity's purpose.

Like yesterday's passage, today's verses describe creation (again), but this scene zooms in on the garden of Eden. First we see lovely trees, a river, and mist gently watering the earth from the ground (Genesis 2:5-9). God also made a man from the ground and gave him a mission (vv. 7-8).
- What did this mission include, according to Genesis 2:15 and Genesis 2:19? How does this relate to the human dominion and fruitfulness we read about in Genesis 1:28?

Work was a part of God's good design. Working alone, however, was not good. God said, *"It is not good that the man should be alone; I will make him a helper fit for him"* (Genesis 2:18).

The Hebrew word for "*helper*" here is *ezer*. In English, "helper" may sound subservient in a negative way to some of us, but in Hebrew, it's worth noting that an *ezer* is someone who supports by providing great strength and value. Scripture describes God Himself as an *ezer* for Israel in verses like Genesis 49:25, Deuteronomy 33:26, Psalm 33:20 and Isaiah 41:13. And in scriptures about warfare, *ezer* often refers to a powerful ally (see Joshua 10:33 and 2 Samuel 8:5 for examples).

The description of Eve as "*fit*" for Adam is also interesting (Genesis 2:18). In Hebrew, *neged* ("*fit*") means "that which is opposite, that which corresponds … like his opposite … proper for him."[1] God made Eve using a rib from the man's side (Genesis 2:21), which suggests she was made to stand at his side.[2] She wasn't made from his head, which may have implied rulership over him; she also wasn't made from his feet, which may have implied inferiority to him.[3] Man and woman are meant to stand side by side as partners and co-workers in God's Kingdom (Genesis 1:27).
- Look at today's passage again, and write down any new insights you see based on these Hebrew meanings of "helper" and "fit."

The relationship between "*man*" and "*wife*" in Genesis 2:24-25 goes on to describe a special form of intentional partnership between men and women: marriage. Within this partnership, three things are meant to happen:

1. A man (husband) leaves his father and mother (v. 24).

2. He "*hold[s] fast to his wife,*" and they become "*one flesh*" (v. 24).

3. Together, both spouses can be naked and unashamed (v. 25).

Underlying the beautiful relationship is this phrase: *"naked and ... not ashamed"* (v. 25). Adam and Eve existed together with full awareness of one another — no hiding, no covering, no secrets. Sex within the boundaries of godly marriage was and is a part of God's good design.* In such bold vulnerability, there is meant to be no shame.

- In today's readings from the creation account, we see that work, sex and marriage were and are all part of God's design. Do any of these surprise you? Why or why not?

This part of Genesis describes perfect, flourishing relationships. It gives us a peek into a reality that was complete and whole, as yet unbroken.

Today, our relationships, even the very best ones, have elements of brokenness and exist in brokenness (we'll discuss why later in this week's study). But reading God's plan for relationships is meant to tug at our hearts and make us long for more.

- Which relationships tug most at your heart and create longing (for instance: relationships with parents, children, spouse, etc.)?

- Write down a few places where your current relationships are broken. Prayerfully ask God to heal each situation.

> *Sex is designed to be a beautiful intimacy between husband and wife. If you feel unsafe, unloved or ashamed during sex, please reach out to a trusted counselor. There is hope; God can restore even the places that feel the most broken.*

Day 3 - GENESIS 3:1-13
Humans disobeyed and undermined God's order.

The story of Genesis takes a downward turn in Chapter 3. A serpent approached Eve and pointed out that the tree God told her not to eat from in Genesis 2:17 could make her wise.

There is a quick progression of verbs here as Eve "**saw** that the tree was good ... **desired** [it] to make one wise ... **took** of its fruit and **ate**" (Genesis 3:6, emphases added). This sentence is so quick after the slow and descriptive chapters before. We almost want to reach out and grab her arm — but there's no time.

What was it that Eve wanted? The serpent told her the tree in the middle of the garden would open her eyes and make her *"like God, knowing good and evil"* (Genesis 3:5). Her longing was to determine good and evil for herself. She, and Adam along with her, wanted to decide what was right and wrong.
- Does that temptation feel real to you too? Where in your life and your relationships have you wanted to be the one who decides what is good and evil — rather than yielding to God's determination?

- Where in your life have you been tempted to know more than God has revealed to you, as if He were withholding something good?

In His perfect order, God had placed Adam and Eve in the garden to bear His image and steward His creation. They wanted more, though. They reached for their own order, wanting to be like God Himself. This moment is often referenced as "the fall" of humanity, when sin entered the world (Romans 5:12). To sin, as defined by Adam and Eve's choice in the garden, is to attempt equality with God, to reject His authority and decide what is right and wrong for ourselves.

- In Genesis 3:7, what was the first thing that happened after Adam and Eve ate from the tree?

Their decision to sin resulted in a breach in their relationship. No longer was vulnerability comfortable, as in Genesis 2:25. Now it was necessary to cover up, to hide. Their partnership would never again be the same.
- Who else did Adam and Eve hide from in Genesis 3:8-10?

We all have felt shame and the compulsion to hide. We can easily put ourselves in the emotional place of Adam and Eve. Shame, unfortunately, is universal to the human experience. It wasn't supposed to be though. Before Adam and Eve *saw, desired, took* and *ate*, there was no shame between them, and there was no shame between them and God.
- We all have struggled with shame in our lives in one way or another. How can you ask God to help you be honest with Him about your feelings and not hide them or hide *from* them?

- Let's go back to those places of temptation we wrote down in answering the first questions on this day of study. Would you dare to vulnerably hold those up to God and ask Him to shed His light of wisdom? Below, write a short prayer inviting God to give you a fresh perspective and fresh start.

Day 4 - GENESIS **3:14-21**
God cursed the serpent and the ground and gave consequences to humanity.

When Adam and Eve sinned, they undermined God's order for creation. The curses and consequences for sin would directly affect every good thing God had intended for them — and us — to enjoy with ease. Let's look at three areas of life that were once thriving and cooperative but are now filled with strife and pain.

1. FAMINE/PROVISION.
   - Adam and Eve were originally tasked to steward a world that flourished (Genesis 1:28-29; Genesis 2:15). But now how does sin affect this stewardship, according to Genesis 3:17-19?

In the ANE context, the phrase translated as *"by the sweat of your face"* in Genesis 3:19 did not necessarily mean hotter sun or harder work. Rather, it described anxious fear because failure and death were real possibilities, and flourishing was not a given.[1] Famine, food scarcity and hunger were and are now part of the world.

2. FERTILITY.
   - Adam and Eve were originally blessed and told to be fruitful and multiply (Genesis 1:28). But now how does sin affect this fruitfulness, according to Genesis 3:16a?

The word *"pain"* here in Genesis 3:16 communicates both the physical agony of childbirth and the emotional "torture of a struggle that has no guaranteed outcome, which may bring life or fail in death."[2] The beauty of childbirth now comes with pain, which can include infertility, discomfort in nursing, pain in giving birth, and other struggles, even the tragedy of mortality. When we experience such pains, God weeps with us in our heartbreak (Psalm 34:18). He knows better than anyone that our world is not supposed to be this way.

3. FAMILY.
- Adam and Eve were a perfect fit, designed to live in a cohesive and cooperative marriage (Genesis 2:24-25). But now how does sin affect this relationship, according to what God told Eve in Genesis 3:16b?

God's perfect order had Adam and Eve working together to rule over animals (Genesis 1:26). Ruling was not designed as a tug-of-war between two image bearers. But after Adam and Eve chose *their order* instead of God's, relationships, particularly between man and woman, became subject to power struggles and manipulation instead of unity and collaboration.

These three areas of brokenness have impacted us all in one way or another. Since the first people tried to declare autonomy from God, anxious fear, family difficulties and relational dysfunction have caused disorder in God's perfect creation.

Even still … God reacted with blessing despite the brokenness Adam and Eve initiated.
- Adam and Eve were exiled. But as they left Eden, what did God give them in Genesis 3:21?

- Has your sin ever made you feel too far from God? How have you seen God respond with blessing even when you've made a mess?

- In all the brokenness, is humanity still made in God's image? How so? Turn to Genesis 9:6, 1 Corinthians 15:49 and Romans 8:29 as you consider your answer.

This is the story of creation, and it's the story of Genesis: Over and over, people act in ways that are right in their own eyes, perpetually "looking out for No. 1" (themselves). And over and over, God sees, acts and blesses.

Is God still a good God when everything's broken? Genesis says **yes**.

Day 5 – GENESIS 3:22-24

Adam and Eve were forced to leave Eden, exiled because of their disobedience.

In the ancient world, people told stories of the human struggle to access the gods or eternal life. They often believed the gods were just beyond reach and eternal life was impossible to earn.

This is not so far off from many people's beliefs today. In the 21st century, views about God's inaccessibility have different names, like "agnosticism" (which says there may be a God, but we will never know), "atheism" (which says there isn't a God), or even "cultural" religious practices (association with a religion's rituals or history without actually believing in the named faith). Many assume God is inaccessible — and should we be interested in finding Him, it will be difficult and yield mixed results.

But when God placed humanity in His garden, He expressed His desire for humanity to live *with Him*.
- Where was the tree of life, according to Genesis 2:9? (Was it accessible or inaccessible?)

- Where did God walk, according to Genesis 3:8? (Was He accessible or inaccessible?)

Heaven and earth collided in Eden. There was no need to travel or search for God; He was right there. God created humanity with eternal life and access to Him. God and eternity were not ours to find — they were ours to lose.

And sadly, we did.

In our reading today, God sent Adam and Eve (and with them, all humanity) out from the garden of Eden. They were no longer allowed access to the tree of life, which was both an act of discipline and an act of mercy so they would not live forever in their state of brokenness (Genesis 3:22).

It might seem that here, when humanity chose our own order over God's, the story of Scripture would be over, with a not-so-happy ending. But there's a whole lot of the Bible left!

Let's jump ahead to the very last book of the Bible to see where God will take the story.
- Revelation 21-22 describes a new heaven and new earth. In what ways is this place, and God's presence in it, similar to Eden? Compare Genesis 2:9-14 and Genesis 3:8 with Revelation 21:1-4 and Revelation 22:1-5.

God's good and ordered creation began with humanity working and living in His presence, and that's what will happen again for God's people in eternity.

So what is God's plan for this restoration and redemption? The answers are in the pages of the Bible between Genesis 3 and Revelation 21.

The Bible repeats stories of human exile and of God's rescue and restoration — and each time God has rescued His people, He has enabled them to dwell closer and closer with Him. In the book of Exodus, for example, God saved His people from slavery in Egypt and taught them how to live lives that reflected Him. He set up a temple and dwelled among them. And today when we trust in His Son, Jesus, God saves us from slavery to sin and death, and Jesus shows us what it means to live for His Kingdom.
- Read 1 Corinthians 3:16 and Romans 8:8-10. Now that Jesus has lived, died and resurrected, where is the new temple, or the dwelling place of God?

God made humanity to be able to function as a temple so His Holy Spirit could live inside us. His desire has always been restoration and dwelling with humankind.
- Reread Genesis 3:22-24 with a focus on God's mercy, and below, spend some time writing words of thanks to God that He is a God of rescue and restoration.

WEEK ONE
Reflection

A solid understanding of the first three chapters of Genesis helps us frame the rest of the Bible. These scriptures answer the questions:

- What is God's intention for the world?
- What does His good order look like?
- What temptations does humanity face?
- How does God interact with those who undermine His order?

Most of all, the creation account in Genesis 1-3 points to the standard God set for how the world *should* function, which tethers the stories in the rest of His Word. The text sets up a picture of God's good world and demonstrates His goodness. It shows us He holds power and authority without insecurity or vindictiveness. He made a good garden because His delight is to create good things, give good tasks and dwell with humanity.

These character qualities underlie all of God's actions. We can always rest in the character He has demonstrated from the beginning.

I praise You, God, for being the Creator of a *beautiful* and *good* world. Thank You for demonstrating Your *delight* in us and Your desire to *dwell* with us. Forgive me for where I have chosen my way over Yours. Please teach me to *trust* that Your plans are *always* best and that You will *always* lead me to what is *good*, not bad. May I continue to see Your *abundant* blessings in this broken world, even while I wait for You to make all things new once more. In Jesus' name, *amen*.

NOTES

NOTES

WEEK
Two

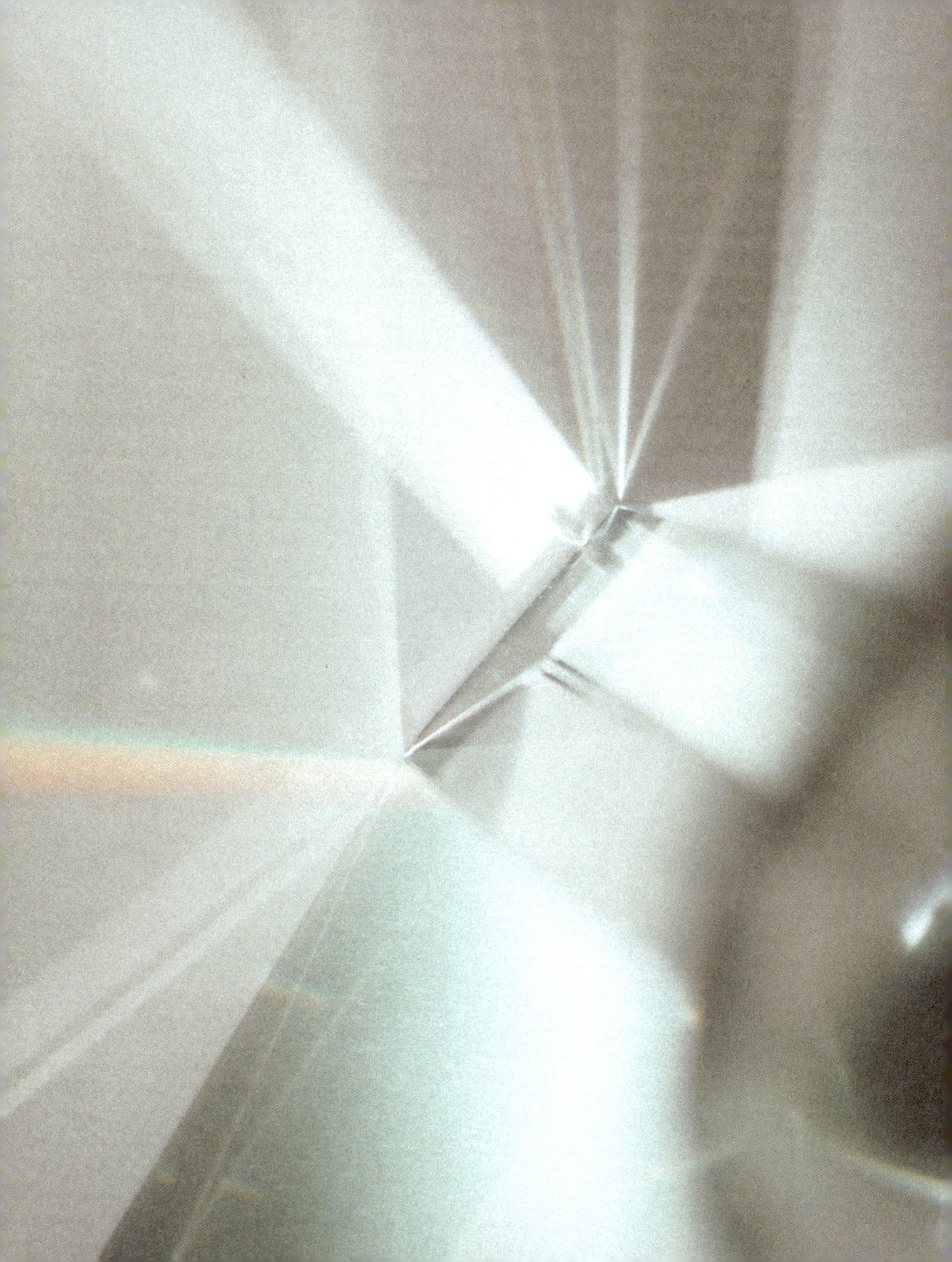

Day 6 – GENESIS 4:1-16

Cain and Abel revealed the consequences of envy and murder.

Adam and Eve had two sons, Cain and Abel. When each son brought offerings to God, God was pleased with Abel's offering and not with Cain's, which made Cain angry and jealous (Genesis 4:3-5). Scholars and commentators debate why God liked or disliked each offering – but even while we may not fully understand all the reasons, we can be sure Cain knew what was in his own heart as he gave his offering, and so did God.

With this in mind, there are several truths we can learn about both God and humanity from today's reading.

- After God saw Cain's anger, He spoke directly to Cain, warning him. In Genesis 4:7, what was the warning?

  "If you do well" …

  "If you do not do well" …

- What did God tell Cain about the nature of sin in Genesis 4:7? How does this apply to our lives today?

Unfortunately, Cain did not heed God's warning. He designed and executed a plan to murder his brother (v. 8). Sin crouched at the door and then pounced, fulfilling its desire with Cain's murderous blows.

The next scene has a rhythm similar to that of God's conversation with Adam and Eve after they disobeyed Him in Genesis 3:9-13. God asked Cain where Abel was, and Cain had the audacity to lie to God, then claimed in Genesis 4:9 that it was not his job to know where Abel was.

God responded decisively, telling Cain he would become a *"fugitive"* and be *"cursed from the ground"* (Genesis 4:11-12). Cain's interactions with the ground would no longer produce fruit (as when he had enough to present an offering of fruit in verse 3); now, the ground would not give Cain its best.

Terrified, Cain claimed this punishment was too much to bear. As a lone wanderer on the earth, he was sure he would be easy prey. Ironically, the first murderer was afraid he would be murdered (v. 14).

- What was God's response to Cain's fears in Genesis 4:15? What does this response reveal about God's character? (For instance, does it show justice? Goodness? Mercy?)

This first scene outside the garden of Eden reveals much. While introducing the theme of brotherly/family discord that permeates the rest of Genesis, these verses also teach us about God's perspective on sin, God's expectations of our responsibilities to each other, and God's bent toward mercy.

In Genesis 4:7, God described sin like an animal lurking at the door of a tent, with Cain as the prey, made vulnerable by his anger.[1] But there was a second part: Cain was not a victim without hope of survival. God urged Cain to master (*"rule over"*) sin. Sin is dangerous, to be sure, but it does not have the ability to dominate us without our permission.

We also see that God was intimately involved in the brothers' relationships. He saw Cain's interactions with Abel and observed when Cain's anger was simmering. Cain's jealousy was about his offering to the Lord, but God focused on how the jealousy affected Cain. Finally, Abel's blood cried out to God from the ground (v. 10). God was involved in observing His people, warning them against sin and delivering justice.

Just as He did in the garden, God met human guilt with judgment *and* grace.[2] Cain was expelled *and* received a mark of protection to save him from the very actions he had committed (Genesis 4:15). How does God's perspective on sin, based on Genesis 4, affect your own perspective?

- Take a minute to list out any relationships that are causing you distress, jealousy or anger today. Prayerfully ask God to show you ways of peace.

Day 7 – GENESIS **4:17-5:32**

A lineage from Adam to Noah marked the passing of many generations.

Today's scriptures are again about a set of brothers — Cain and Seth — but instead of telling a story about their interactions, this time the Bible follows their genealogies.

Sometimes these long lists of names can feel a little monotonous. Tucked inside these lists, though, are insights into how humanity was growing and changing.
- Take a look at Cain's genealogy in Genesis 4:17-22, and write down all the occupations or types of work you see listed.

- According to Genesis 4:23-24, what happened with Lamech in Cain's genealogy?

Cain's family had diverse occupations, and perhaps because of their inability to farm after the curse of Genesis 4:11-12, they developed wonderful skills in artistry. But Lamech revealed a darker side. The fear of a violent death — and the impulse to murder in anger — still ran through Cain's family, so much so that a poem about Lamech's revenge philosophy was passed down. Violence spread just as the advancement of humanity spread, and the good and bad were held in tension.
- Next, Seth's genealogy reveals an interesting time marker. Who did people "beg[in] to call upon" when Seth's son was born (Genesis 4:26)? Why is this significant?

- Read Genesis 5:21-24. What made Enoch's entry in the family tree unique?

Seven generations in, Enoch's life contrasted to the rest of the family tree. He was noted for his unique relationship with God and for the end of his earthly journey: Genesis 5:24 links Enoch's "wal[k] with God" to his exit directly into God's presence. Hebrews 11:5 says, "Enoch was taken up [by God] so that he should not see death."

- In Genesis 5:25, a Lamech from Seth's family (not the Lamech of Genesis 4:23-24) entered the family tree. What did Lamech name his son, according to Genesis 5:28-29? Why?

It doesn't take a close reading to see many years had passed since Adam and Eve left the garden. People had been toiling for generations because of the curse of sin. Old Testament scholar Iain Provan notes, "Lamech [was] not merely anticipating *comfort* in the midst of painful toil, then, but looking for *relief* from the cursing of the ground mentioned in Genesis 3:17."[1]

This Lamech was not seeking revenge. Between the cursed ground and the evil hearts of humans, he just wanted relief. He didn't want a hug or a cup of hot cocoa; he wanted the curse to lift and ease everyone's burden.

We've probably all had similar times when we get tired of platitudes and even of genuine sympathy in the midst of hardship, times when we simply long for our pain to disappear. In many ways, we can empathize with Lamech's hopes.

Keeping our empathy for Lamech's plea in mind, as we peruse all the numbers listed in today's verses, we see there are so *many* generations and years between Adam and Lamech! God was patiently letting humans move along … in the way they wanted … for a very long time. Although this "moving along" included ever-increasing sin, God was not capricious or vindictive, jumping on every mistake. And still today, we hold in tension our longing for relief from sin and our gratitude for God's patience with us as sinners (2 Peter 3:9).
- Let's close out today in prayer, thanking God for His long patience with humanity and also asking for relief from things that are weighing us down. Holding both of these realities, allow God into your tension. He will meet you there.

Day 8 – GENESIS **6-9**

God saved Noah and his family from the waters of the great flood.

In family-friendly depictions of Noah's ark, we often see animals lining up two by two, boarding a big boat with an elderly gentleman and his wife standing at the door. Birds appear in the clear sky above blue waves below ...

As adults, we see the story of Noah is not so mild. It stands as a dark moment in history. While it had a happy ending of sorts, the journey was fraught.

God had commissioned humanity to multiply (Genesis 1:28), and Genesis 6:1 says they did. However, they were not multiplying as a reflection of a good God, a good Creator, the Author of good order. Instead, as they multiplied, they descended into depravity.

- How did God view the hearts of humans according to Genesis 6:5? How did God view the earth in Genesis 6:11-12?

- How did God *feel* about the state of humanity and creation (Genesis 6:6-7)?

God's good creation was being ruined by humankind. Just as God responded to Cain's murder of Abel (Genesis 4:10-12), He responded again to the darkness that was invading the earth. Judgment came in the form of a flood that overwhelmed the land. But the God who delivered this judgment was and is a good God, who also delivered righteous Noah and made a way to give His creation a fresh start (Genesis 6:18-20).

After the flood, creation was reborn. God blessed Noah and his family, giving them the same command He had given to Adam and Eve: They were to *"be fruitful and multiply"* and fill the earth (Genesis 9:1; Genesis 9:7).

- Reread Genesis 7, and then imagine stepping off the ark into a washed-clean world after the flood. What's the first thing you would do? (For example: cook a hot meal, start building a house, take a walk on solid ground for the first time in months, etc.)

The first thing Noah did was worship God. Noah built an altar and offered burnt offerings, and God was pleased. He established a covenant with Noah, Noah's sons and the earth itself (Genesis 8:20-22).
- What was the covenant promise God made to Noah in Genesis 9:11? What was the sign of the promise in verses 13-16?

In both English and Hebrew, the word for "*bow*" in Genesis 9:13 is the same as the word for the weapon (i.e., a bow and arrow).[1] When God placed the bow in the sky, He placed it facing the heavens, like a warrior holding the bow at rest — not drawn back, ready to fire. In a sense, this placement represented a ceasing of hostility between God and humanity.[2] It was a declaration of peace.
- How does your understanding of the rainbow change when you think of it as a bow *pointed away* from you? When have you thought God's arrow was drawn at you, and how does the rainbow reveal His peace?

- In Genesis 6:5, God said *"every intention of the thoughts of [the human] heart was only evil continually."* Did the flood solve this problem? What does Genesis 8:21 reveal about the heart?

As Lamech hoped in Genesis 5:29, Noah did bring relief from the curse — but it may not have been as Lamech envisioned. Instead of fixing the world as it was, God brought a clean slate and fresh start. After the flood, all of creation was reborn, and God made new everlasting commitments to all of creation.
- Reflect on the promises you've made to other people or the ones people have made to you. How is your life impacted by knowing that God *will not* and *cannot* break His covenant (2 Timothy 2:13)?

LITERARY CHIASM *of* THE STORY *of* NOAH

Remember how we talked about the literary technique of chiasm at the beginning of this study guide? (Turn back to Page 17 for a refresher!) Below is an outline of what some scholars see as the chiastic structure of the story of Noah and the flood.[1] Notice how this structure places emphasis on God's faithfulness as the most important, central part of the account.

Transition from the generations before Noah (Genesis 6:9-10).

    Sin and violence corrupted God's creation (Genesis 6:11-12).

        God addressed Noah, resolving to destroy the fallen world (Genesis 6:13-22).

            God addressed Noah, commanding that he enter the ark (Genesis 7:1-10).

                The flood began (Genesis 7:11-16).

                    The floodwaters rose (Genesis 7:17-24).

                    God remembered Noah (Genesis 8:1a).

                    The floodwaters receded (Genesis 8:1b-5).

                The earth dried (Genesis 8:6-14).

            God addressed Noah, commanding that he leave the ark (Genesis 8:15-19).

        God resolved to preserve the recreated world (Genesis 8:20-22).

    God addressed Noah and humanity in a covenant of peace (Genesis 9:1-17).

Transition to the generations after Noah (Genesis 9:18-19).

Day 9 - GENESIS **10-11:26**

The tower of Babel incident resulted in the scattering of humanity.

After the flood of Genesis 6-9, the next genealogy lists what was at the time the entire known world: 70 nations descended through Noah's three sons, Japheth, Ham and Shem (Genesis 10:1-31). Japheth's descendants were kin groups who occupied modern-day Turkey, spreading both east and west. Ham's descendants inhabited places from the Arabian Gulf through Canaan and into northern Africa. Shem's family covered the land to the east and south of Israel.[1]

The original readers of Genesis, ancient Israelites, would have recognized the names and places listed in these genealogies just as we recognize important historical figures and regions today (like George Washington or Martin Luther King Jr., the East Coast or the Great Plains).

- According to Genesis 10:25, what happened to the earth when Peleg was alive? How might this relate to Genesis 11:8-9?

The story of Babel in Genesis 11 may have taken place during Peleg's time. At some point beforehand, all people spoke one language, and everyone moved as a group (Genesis 11:1-2). Then one day the people were living on a plain and planned to build a tower with an expressed goal: *"Let us make a name for ourselves, lest we be dispersed over the face of the whole earth"* (Genesis 11:4).

- Based on God's words in Genesis 1:28 and Genesis 9:7, were people supposed to live all in one place? Why or why not? What does this reveal about the people's refusal to *"be dispersed over the face of the whole earth"* in Genesis 11:4?

- Where would the top of their tower reach toward (Genesis 11:4)? What might this reveal about their motivations for building it?

Archaeologists have found pyramid-like towers called ziggurats in the Mesopotamian region that claimed their "foundations were in the underworld and [their] top reached the heavens."[2] At the top of these towers were temples for the gods.

The story of the tower of Babel reveals a different perspective about how high a human tower could actually go. Genesis 11:5 notes, *"The LORD came down to see the city and the tower, which the children of man had built,"* a bit of a poke at the idea that the tower reached heaven. It must not have been very high if God had to *come down* to see it!

- According to Genesis 11:9, why was the city named Babel? (If your Bible has a footnote about the word "Babel" here, read that too!)

God didn't engage in tower wars, knocking down the people's tower for them to rebuild it. Instead, He confused their language. There's even a subtle play on words here, as the Hebrew word meaning "confuse" sounds like "Babel." Additionally, to the locals in Babylonia, the word *babil* meant "gate of god."[3] Their so-called gate of god was met with confusion.

This story started when the people wanted a tower to God and a name for themselves — but they ended up with a half-built city named after a pun for "confusion." It's likely the initial hearers of this story gave a bit of a chortle.

Like Adam and Eve, the people in Genesis 11 wanted to decide what was good and evil. They ignored God's instructions and the good order He had set forth. And like expulsion from the garden prevented Adam and Eve from accessing the tree of life in their sinful state (Genesis 3:22-24), the variation of languages served as God's mercy toward the people at Babel, thwarting their determination to build one immoral civilization (Genesis 11:7-8).

- Today humans continue to build metaphorical "towers" of pride and make names for ourselves instead of acting as God's image in all the earth. Where do you see examples of this today?

- When have you experienced negative consequences of a prideful or unwise decision in your own life, only to find that this was also God's mercy preventing you from continuing in a worse direction?

Day 10 - GENESIS 11:27-12:9

God called Abram.

Our reading today marks a major pivot in Genesis. Thus far, our stories have been about the history of the world; now, the narrative narrows to focus on the history of Israel.

Genesis 11:10-27 tells us that from the line of Noah's son Shem came a man named Terah. Along with his son Abram; Abram's wife, Sarai; and his orphaned nephew, Lot, Terah moved from Ur (near Babylon, or modern-day Iraq) to Haran (near modern-day Turkey).

After Terah's death, God spoke to Abram in Genesis 12:1-3 and made a covenant with him. In this covenant, Abram had a part to play, and so did God.

- Fill in the blank to identify Abram's part: "_____ from your country and your kindred and your father's house to the land that [God] will show you" (Genesis 12:1).

- Fill in the blanks to identify God's part: "And I will _____ of you a great nation, and I will _____ you and _____ your name great, so that you will be a blessing. I will _____ those who bless you, and him who dishonors you I will _____, and in you all the families of the earth shall be blessed" (Genesis 12:2-3).

After reading Genesis thus far, we are ready for this fresh start! Since Genesis 3, the story has gone from bad to worse with only a few bright spots. But suddenly there seems to be a plan for Abram. Without any sort of preamble about his righteousness, like we read with Enoch (Genesis 5:24) or Noah (Genesis 6:9), God called Abram. God told him to walk.

- What did Abram do, and who went with him, in Genesis 12:4-5?

- When Abram got to the oak of Moreh at Shechem in verse 7, what did the Lord promise?

Abram ... well, he walked. He acted in obedience with nothing but the (pretty incredible!) promise of family and land on the other side. As we read about yesterday, at Babel, a group of people wanted to *make their own name great*. In Genesis 12, God said *He would make Abram's name great* so he could be a blessing.

This was a fresh start, indeed. And God wasn't only making a promise to Abram or calling a nation (Israel) into existence. He was doing much more: He was laying out His redemption plan to bless *"all the families of the earth"* (Genesis 12:3). The same God who called the world into existence called Abram to follow Him in faith ... and He calls you and me to do the same today.[1]

- Twice in today's reading, the Lord promised Abram a family with many descendants (Genesis 12:2; Genesis 12:7). Why was this surprising, according to Genesis 11:30?

For the first step in the redemption plan, God called a broken man in a broken world to have faith in Him. All Abram had to do was *go*. With great faith, Abram believed God's promise and took both literal and spiritual steps of obedience.

Sometimes we make faith out to be complicated. It can feel risky, and it requires boldness. But in many ways, it's actually not complicated: God calls each of us to believe Him and His promises.
- Where is God calling you to go in faith (literally or metaphorically)? Have you been obedient, or have you delayed obedience (which is disobedience) because you don't know where He's taking you? Will you choose to believe He is trustworthy?

MAP OF **ABRAHAM'S JOURNEY**

Below is a map of the Fertile Crescent, which consists of Canaan, Egypt and Mesopotamia (the land between the Tigris River and Euphrates River). The Fertile Crescent is named for its shape as well as its proximity to water that allowed crops and livestock to thrive. Abraham's journey is marked by arrows, starting near the Persian Gulf (Ur) and extending all the way to Egypt. You'll also see the names and locations of some other cities and locations we'll encounter in Genesis (like Shechem, Gerar and Goshen).

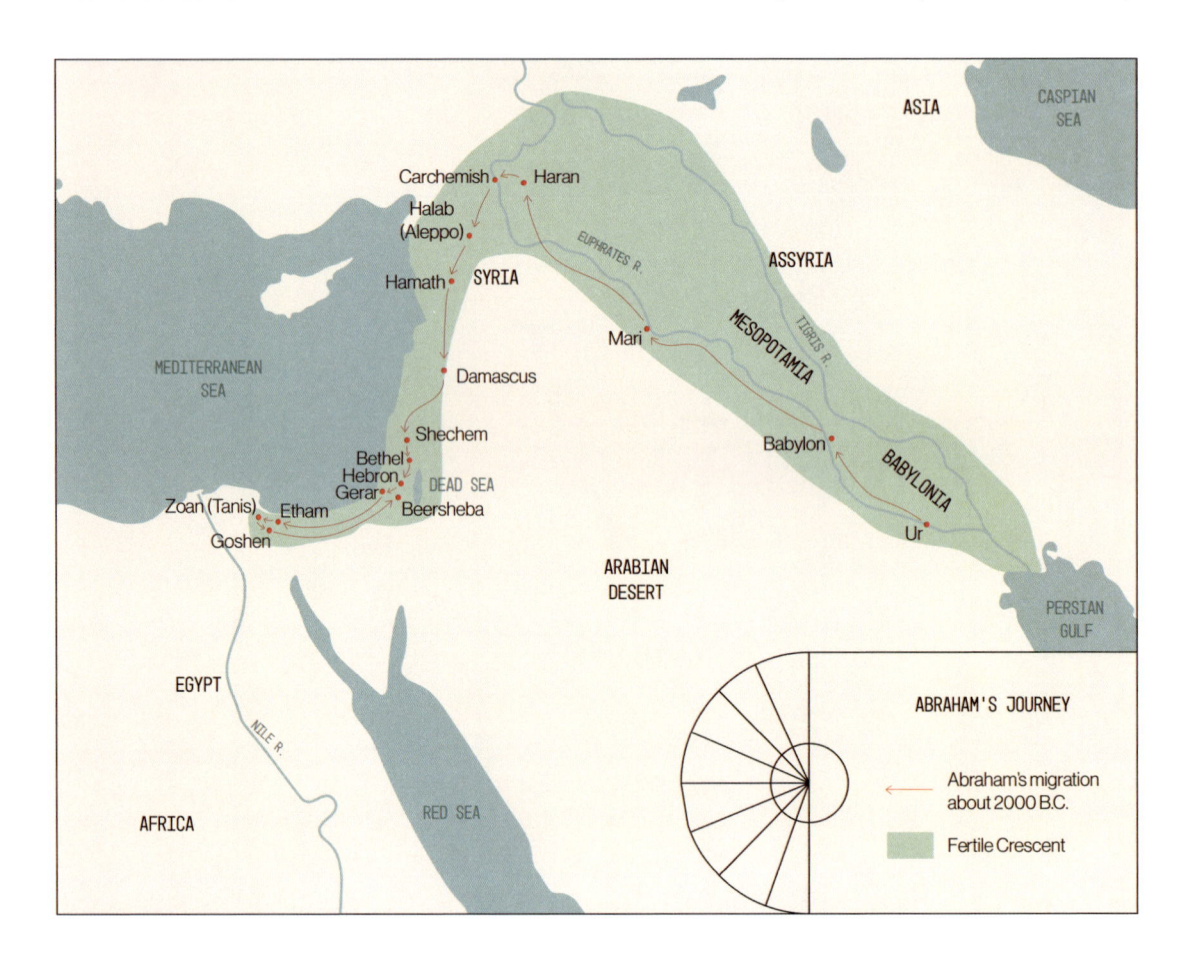

WEEK **TWO**
Reflection

Imagine for a minute that you've never heard any of the Genesis story before. Or maybe you don't have to imagine, and through this study, you're taking in these true stories for the first time. Either way, Genesis is designed to draw us in.

We're meant to stand in awe at God's majesty and power in creation — then we feel the devastation as God walked in the garden and called for sinful Adam and Eve (Genesis 1-3). We are gobsmacked when we see how God gently warned Cain and rooted for him to "*do well*" (Genesis 4:7). We wonder what God would do when every human's intention was evil and God was grieved to His heart (Genesis 6:5-6). We are amazed as we witness the way God saved Noah through the flood and gave relief to the earth (Genesis 6-9). After the flood, we shake our heads as we see that instead of filling the earth, humans gathered together and attempted to build a wayward way to heaven (Genesis 11).

The stories from Adam to Noah have a general downward trend, and it might seem Babel was starting another descent. But what about God's actions? God warned Cain, walked with Enoch, grieved evil, honored righteousness, recommissioned Noah's family after the flood, and dispersed people to remind humanity we cannot reach heaven on our own. God was consistent. God did not meet humanity's downward trend with His own. He was patient, He never lost His temper, and He always found ways to bless.

The second part of Genesis starts with this backdrop. Humanity had a regular inclination toward evil, and God was consistently inclined to restore and bless.

Enter: Abram.

With Abram, God started something new. He made a promise to bless the entire world through the family of one man — even though Abram was childless at the time — and then He declared Abram righteous after he chose to obey (Romans 4:3; James 2:23; Galatians 3:6). Here God didn't call a righteous man to action; God called a man and declared that *faith made him righteous*.

Something shifted in Genesis when God made a promise and Abram started walking ... and we still have 38 more chapters for the story to unfold.

Lord, thank You for Your long *patience* and *kindness*. We are grateful for Your *consistent* character. Help us to learn who You are so we can better *follow* You. Help us to listen to Your Word with new ears, hearing it afresh. Show us Your character, and reveal our own downward trends to us. We are grateful for Your *goodness* and *grace*. In Jesus' name, *amen*.

NOTES

NOTES

WEEK
Three

Day 11 - GENESIS **12:10-20**

Abram and his family traveled to Egypt during a famine.

Last week, we were introduced to Abram, a regular guy in the family line of Shem who received an amazing promise from God and acted with faith. As Abram traveled with his family and caravan, they ended up in Egypt, searching for relief from a famine (Genesis 12:10).

When he walked into Egypt, Abram seemed to feel deeply vulnerable. He was a foreigner, and his wife was beautiful, both facts Abram thought put him at risk of death. In the ANE, powerful leaders like Pharaoh often took what and who they wanted by force. Abram claimed he and Sarai were siblings to keep himself safe (Genesis 12:12-13) — but this put Sarai in jeopardy. With a lie, Abram shifted his vulnerability to his wife. "*And the woman was taken into Pharaoh's house*" (v. 15b).
- What did the Lord do in Genesis 12:17?

The Lord protected Sarai when Abram did not. Abram may have felt he was in danger, but the Lord had promised to protect him and his family (Genesis 12:1-3). Just as God watched over Sarai, He would have aided Abram even if he hadn't tried to take matters into his own hands.
- Pharaoh quickly sent Sarai and Abram away with all their things. What did they take with them from Pharaoh (vv. 16, 20)? How does this reveal God's provision?

After reading Genesis 3-11, we might read today's story with bated breath ... then disappointment. Abram started his journey with an act of unusual faith but then acted with cowardice, lying to protect himself. Twelve chapters into Genesis, we might have hoped humanity would produce a worthy hero. But Abram fell short. In fact, we might wonder if his sin would result in another flood or a massive disruption like at Babel.

But God's response to Abram's unfaithfulness was to protect him and Sarai, provide for them, and continue to keep His promise. If the promised blessing depended fully on Abram, we'd be quickly disappointed. But the story of Scripture will never depend on human faithfulness — God and His promises always stand at the center.
- What a relief that God's faithfulness does not depend on us but on His character! Take a minute and write out Psalm 100:5. Consider keeping the written verse in clear view and/or memorizing it this week.

Over and over, God will bless and protect, guide and care for His people. The miracle of Genesis is watching how God gently and consistently taught Abram and his descendants about Himself. He showed them His mercy, His justice, His patience and His faithfulness.

It can seem like the patriarchs are the main characters, but in Genesis (indeed, in the entire Bible), the true main character is God. As we continue to witness the patriarchs' journeys, we'll see them either faithfully serving a faithful God or proving God's faithfulness despite their own disobedience and doubts.

We get the privilege of a holy eavesdrop, listening to how God taught and guided His people. What a gift!
- Reflect on a time when you messed up but God still took care of you. Take a moment to praise God for His faithfulness.

- Ask God if there is any situation in your life right now where you are doubting He will come through for you. Write a prayer that He will give you the boldness to trust His faithfulness and to depend on His character more than your abilities.

Day 12 - GENESIS **13-14**

Abram and Lot parted ways.

After some poor decisions in Egypt, Abram, Sarai, Lot and their caravan traveled north toward Bethel and Ai. On this journey, Abram and his family would have crossed the desert and some fairly intense terrain. The distance from Egypt to Bethel/Ai is roughly the equivalent of the distance from Charlotte, NC, to Virginia Beach, VA, or from Phoenix, AZ, to Las Vegas, NV. Though this trip takes up just a few sentences in our Bibles (Genesis 13:3-4), it took much time and effort for Abram's family. Assuming the "ancient average of 15 miles per day," scholars estimate this would have taken a minimum of 20-22 days if they went nonstop.[1]

- Go back to the map on Page 54, and track Abram's journey this far. Maybe highlight or trace the route between Egypt and Bethel/Ai. If you're feeling creative, also look up the city you live in and map the route to a city 300-350 miles away. What do you think it would be like to walk this distance with your extended family, a small business and a bunch of animals?

Abram and Lot had so much property and livestock they eventually needed to split up because their herdsmen weren't getting along. Abram knew they needed to divide their land to maintain peace, and he gave Lot the first pick. Naturally, Lot chose what looked best (Genesis 13:5-11).

Healthy land was incredibly important to sustain any ANE family and their property. By giving Lot the first pick, Abram showed more faith here than he had in Egypt. He wasn't acting from fear but was acting as a man who knew his future was secure because of God's promises.

Apparently pleased with this generosity, God made even more promises to Abram.

- Fill in the blanks from Genesis 13:14-17, paying close attention to who these promises depended on:

    "Lift up your eyes and look from the place where you are, northward and southward and eastward and westward, for all the land that you see _____ _____ give to you and to your offspring forever. _____ _____ make your offspring as the dust of the earth, so that if one can count the dust of the earth, your offspring also can be counted. Arise, walk through the length and the breadth of the land, for _____ _____ give it to you."

The story continued as Lot was taken hostage by enemies, and then Abram rescued him (Genesis 14:1-16). After the battle and victory, Abram was met by two kings.

- The king of Sodom did not offer anything to Abram. What did the king of Salem (Melchizedek) offer? What did he say to Abram in Genesis 14:18-20?

The king of Sodom was terse and rude, showing uncharacteristically inhospitable behavior for the region. Abram had done the king a favor by rescuing his people and recovering stolen goods, and presumably Abram had a claim to some of what he had recouped. But he seemed to sense that he ultimately did not need anything from the king of Sodom and chose instead to depend on *"the LORD, God Most High, Possessor of heaven and earth"* (Genesis 14:22).

- Do you think you would have responded to the king as Abraham did in Genesis 14:21-24? Why or why not?

- When you are tempted toward a scarcity mindset (focusing on lack, fear and insufficiency), how can you instead trust God to provide, even before the situation has turned around?

Day 13 - GENESIS 15

God established a covenant with Abram.

In today's scriptures, the Lord appeared to Abram in a dream and made another promise to him. This time God declared, *"I am your shield; your reward shall be very great"* (Genesis 15:1), affirming, as we saw yesterday, that Abram didn't need protection or treasure from other nations. God Himself would provide for and guard Abram and his family.

- How else does the promise in Genesis 15:1 compare to the other promises we have seen God make to Abram so far (Genesis 12:1-3; Genesis 13:14-17)?

- For the first time in the Genesis story, Abram responded to God with a question. What did he ask in Genesis 15:2-3?

Abram was certainly grateful for God's protection, but to what end? When he died, his land and provision, all that God had promised him, would go not to a son (because he had no son) but to a designated heir.

God replied, *"This man shall not be your heir; your very own son shall be your heir"* (Genesis 15:4). The phrase *"your very own son"* could also be translated "what will come from your own loins." God wasn't saying an adopted son is not a real son (see Ephesians 1 for proof that God is a huge fan of adoption!), but Abram's family was going to come from a miraculous pregnancy and birth. Not only was a son going to come from Abram's own body, but Abram's descendants would be more than he could count — more numerous than the stars (Genesis 15:5).

- Every time Abram looked at the night sky, he had a lovely reminder of God's promise to him. What's something you see frequently that serves as a reminder of God's promises to you in Scripture? (Consider these verses for a few promises: Matthew 11:28, John 6:35, Hebrews 8:12, Revelation 21:6.)

After his interaction with God in Genesis 15, Scripture makes a profound statement about Abram.
- Write out Genesis 15:6 below. What stands out to you in this statement?

Abram believed God. He did not just agree that God could do the miraculous, but he believed that God *would*. He believed that God was faithful to His promises, that He was good and would bring about His good plan. This wasn't just a mental exercise. As one scholar observes, "He *trusted* himself and his family to the God whom he believed to be good, and he lived his life accordingly."[1]

In response, God acknowledged that act of faith and *"counted it to him as righteousness"* (v. 6). Abram wasn't someone righteous who then acted with faith. His faith counted as his righteousness.
- In the New Testament, the Apostle Paul also wrote about Abram. Read Romans 4:18-25, where he homed in on Abram's trust. Referring back to Genesis 15:6, Romans 4:23-24 says, *"the words 'it was counted to him' were not written for [Abram's] sake alone, but for ..."* who else's sake? Why?

Just as faith was the deciding factor in Abram's relationship with God, so it is in ours. God has been consistent across both the Old and New Testaments: All that is required for a relationship with Him is the belief that He can do what He says He will do and that He is who He says He is.

Abram believed God could create life in his barren family, and he lived accordingly.

We can choose to believe that God *"raised from the dead Jesus our Lord, who was delivered up for our trespasses and raised for our justification"* (Romans 4:24b-25), and we can live accordingly.

Day 14 - GENESIS 16
God saw and heard Hagar.

Hagar was an Egyptian woman who became a servant to Abram and his wife, Sarai. When Abram and Sarai traveled to Egypt, Hagar likely joined them in a slave trade, never having her own autonomy (Genesis 12:16). Abram and Sarai's God was likely not her god. Their ways were not her ways.

In Genesis 16, Sarai begrudged her own infertility and stepped in to move along God's promise of a son for Abram. She offered Hagar to Abram as a means to have a son. This was "normal" behavior in ANE culture — though that doesn't mean God condoned it. In Genesis 2:24, God was clear about His design for faithful marriage between one husband and one wife, and although we see polygamy throughout Genesis, it is never promoted as righteous behavior and frequently caused problems for God's people.

We also don't know how Hagar felt about her situation. Culturally, she may have seen starting a family with Abram as a promotion: The mother of an heir held an elevated position that would have certainly afforded her more privilege and standing. Today, from a modern perspective, we might say Hagar was trafficked. Whether she was happy or sad, we aren't told. But we can probably assume she wasn't asked. And if so, cultural or not, that would have been wrong.
- In the very first chapter of Genesis, God said man and woman are made in His image (Genesis 1:27). By God's decree, all people deserve to be treated with dignity and respect. But sometimes we let the hierarchies of society determine who we value and how much. What are some hierarchies you encounter in your daily life? What does James 2:1-5 say about treating others as more or less valuable because of their position?

Sarai's plan was successful, and Hagar became pregnant. But this created lots of strife in Abram's household. Hagar looked to Sarai with contempt, Sarai complained to Abram, Abram abdicated responsibility, and Sarai treated Hagar harshly (Genesis 16:4-6).

Chaos ensued: Hagar's instinct to lord her pregnancy over Sarai was unkind, to say the least. Sarai's lashing out and using her status as Abram's wife to push Hagar down was straight-up awful.
- What did Hagar do next in Genesis 16:6? Who found her in verse 7?

God sent Hagar back to Sarai to *"submit to her"* (v. 9). In a sense, perhaps He was instructing Hagar to stop her part of the drama (her apparent contempt toward Sarai in verse 4). But it's important to note that God did not approve of how Sarai *"dealt harshly with"* Hagar (v. 6b). This is **not** a prescriptive story for returning to abusive relationships. If you are in a marriage or relationship where you are being harmed, please seek help from a professional counselor. God loves you, and His desire is for you to live in safe and healthy relationships.

In Hagar's unique situation, the Lord told her to go back — but He didn't stop there. He blessed Hagar and told her that she would be the mother of a multitude (vv. 10-12).
- God also told her to name her son Ishmael, which means "God hears." Why did God tell her to name him that, according to verse 11?

God heard every rotten name Hagar may have been called, every time she cried, every time she was sold, traded or treated as a commodity. When He named her son, He reminded her that He was not absent, uninvolved or ambivalent toward her affliction.

Every time Hagar called Ishmael for dinner, she would remind herself and everyone around her that *God heard her.* An Egyptian servant sucked into a foreign land and walking in loneliness was intimately known by God.
- What did Hagar name the Lord in Genesis 16:13?

In the desert, feeling alone and mistreated, Hagar met God. She met Him so personally that they exchanged names: He named her son, and she named Him. Hagar is actually the only person to assign a name to a deity in the entire Old Testament. No longer did Hagar know Him just as Abram's God — He was *her God.* He was the God who found her, saw her and heard her.

So Hagar went back to Abram and Sarai. She carried her own brokenness and sin back into a broken situation with other sinners. But she returned with a blessing and with knowledge of the living God.
- Where have you felt unseen or unheard in your life? Ask God to show you how He has seen or heard you in each situation, and use the space below for journaling or prayer.

Day 15 - GENESIS **17**

God's covenant was solidified with Abram, now called Abraham.

At the beginning of today's scriptures, 13 years had passed since the events of Genesis 16. In those 13 years, while God was presumably silent, Abram raised Ishmael as his son and as the fulfillment of God's promise. And after 13 years, God spoke to Abram again.
- Abram's previous act of obedience was to "*go*" in Genesis 12:1-4. What did God ask him to do this time in Genesis 17:1-2?

In this chapter, God reiterated and added to the Abrahamic covenant. We can segment His declarations here into three sections: promises of what God would do, promises of what Abram would do, and promises of what Sarai would do.
- Working through Genesis 17, fill in the chart below to identify some key promises (noting that some verses may contain more than one promise).

YAHWEH (What was God going to do?)	ABRAM, RENAMED ABRAHAM (What was Abram told to do?)	SARAI, RENAMED SARAH (What was Sarai told to do?)
VERSE **6**:	VERSE **9**:	VERSES **15-16**:
VERSE **7**:	VERSES **10-14**: Circumcise males as a sign of the covenant.	VERSE **19**:
VERSE **8**:	VERSE **19**:	
VERSE **19**: Establish the covenant through Isaac.		
VERSE **20**: Bless Ishmael.		

The past covenant statements in Genesis were expanded. This time, God changed Sarai and Abram's names to Sarah and Abraham (vv. 5, 15), and He said that Abraham would be the father of many nations, that kings would come from Abraham, and that the covenant was "*everlasting*" (vv. 7, 8, 13, 19).

Additionally, God added a sign of this everlasting covenant (just as the rainbow was a sign of His everlasting covenant with Noah in Genesis 9:16). The new sign was circumcision. Among cultures that interacted with Abraham and Sarah, circumcision was a well-known practice used for marriage rites or as a sign of puberty.[1] But God took this known practice and applied it differently. He made it a theological rite, a sign that someone was in a covenant community with Him.

- After God told Abraham that Sarah would have his son, what was Abraham's first response in Genesis 17:17? What was his second response in verse 18?

It's almost as if the realization that Ishmael would not carry the covenant came to Abraham mid-laugh — he quickly went from laughing to protesting. The pivot was so fast it caught him off guard. Even still, *"that very day,"* Abraham, Ishmael and everyone in their household were circumcised (v. 26). Abraham quickly and completely obeyed.

And God heard Abraham's request to bless Ishmael. In the original language, verse 20 reiterates Ishmael's name (meaning "God hears") to show this: *"As for Ishmael, I have heard you"* in Hebrew is *Ishmael ishmael*. Again, Ishmael's very name was a reminder of God's faithfulness. The boy would not be forgotten. In fact, Abraham even included Ishmael in the circumcision, though God would not carry out the covenant through Ishmael's descendants.

God named Abraham's next son Isaac, which meant "he laughs," presumably because the announcement of his miraculous birth was both unbelievable and joyful, making Abraham and Sarah laugh out loud (Genesis 17:17; Genesis 18:12).

- Has God ever done something so delightful that you burst out laughing? It could be good news, a surprise visit, a baby's glee, or even a flower peeking up on a well-worn sidewalk. Recall that moment now, and thank God for His good gifts.

WHAT DOES THE ABRAHAMIC COVENANT MEAN FOR US *Today?*

In the Abrahamic covenant, God included a promise that echoed words He had earlier spoken to Noah and Adam. To Abraham he said, *"I will make you exceedingly fruitful"* (Genesis 17:6). Those same words reverberated 10 generations before when He told Noah, *"Be fruitful and multiply"* (Genesis 9:1; Genesis 9:7). And 10 generations before Noah, God said to Adam and Eve, *"Be fruitful and multiply"* (Genesis 1:28).[1]

Humans have always been called to act as God's representatives on earth. Just as Adam and Eve were made in God's image to steward God's creation, so Noah, made in God's image, was tasked with stewarding the new creation after the flood. Abraham was made in His image, too, and God promised that all nations (filled with more image bearers!) would be blessed through him.

When God spoke to Abraham, it was a major, historic moment of unfolding His plan for salvation through the *"offspring"* He had promised in Genesis 3:15. Abraham carried this promise from God and passed it from generation to generation, a bit like a covenant baton in a relay race. The problem, however, was that Abraham and the other patriarchs carrying the baton struggled mightily to represent Him. They carried the covenant … and sin.

After Genesis, the nation of Israel carried the covenant baton throughout the Old Testament. Their course included mountains of bright joy and valleys of deep darkness. In all of it, God was faithful to Israel, keeping His promise to Abraham (Psalm 106:45).

So God continued to bless all nations through Abraham's lineage, culminating in the arrival of an Israelite named Jesus (Galatians 3:16-18). Jesus is a son of Abraham (Matthew 1:1), and at the same time, He is the *"only Son"* of God (John 3:16)!

Jesus perfectly displays God's character and accurately represents His Kingdom. At last, when Jesus came to earth as God Himself in human form (John 1:14), there was a perfect image bearer carrying the baton for Israel — and for us (Colossians 1:15; 2 Corinthians 4:4; Romans 5:19).

In His sinless life, Jesus showed us how to live as God's representatives; in His death, He "*condemned sin*" that Adam and Eve introduced to the world (Romans 8:3). Like an old building is condemned to be destroyed, sin is demolished by Jesus. Jesus' sacrificial death and resurrection make righteous all who trust in Him, and His Spirit dwells within us (1 Corinthians 6:19).

In Christ, God once again dwells with humanity, just as He dwelled with humanity in the garden of Eden. We are truly blessed indeed!

God called Abraham and made him a huge promise, and Abraham was considered right with God when he believed God would do what He said (Romans 4:23-25; Galatians 3:14; Galatians 3:26). Today God extends a similar invitation to us. He says anyone who believes He raised Jesus from the dead is made right with Him (Romans 4:24). The God who started a plan with Adam, then continued it with Abraham and Israel, fulfilled it with Jesus — and He invites us into that same plan.

All who accept Jesus' invitation are called to walk with God, much like Adam, Enoch and Noah did (Genesis 3:8; Genesis 5:24; Genesis 6:9). Jesus says when we remain connected to Him, He continually transforms us into His image (John 15:4-11; 2 Corinthians 3:18). This blessing would have been beyond Abraham's imagination!

Believers in Jesus now carry the covenant baton (1 Peter 2:9-10). We are blessed by God's faithfulness to Abraham, which ultimately led to Jesus, and we have the abundantly joyful task of blessing others (Matthew 5:16; Ephesians 2:10; Hebrews 10:24). Just as Jesus — God in flesh — stepped into our human pain, we now stand alongside others who are in pain, and along with all of creation, we cry out in the Holy Spirit for full restoration from God (Romans 8:22-27). We believe God will restore everything He has made, bringing renewal to creation just as He has promised (Romans 8:22-25; Revelation 21:1-6; Revelation 22:1-5).

WEEK THREE
Reflection

This week, God's goodness and faithfulness were center stage in our Scripture readings. As a patient Father, He protected Abraham and kept His covenant promises. As a loving Father, He cared for both Sarai and Hagar in their hurt and heartache. These stories, spanning miles and years, portray the God who sees His people and seeks to bless them. He didn't first enter their pain with a mirror to show them their sins and shortcomings; He gave them windows through which they could see Him and not their shame.

All the while, God continued moving the covenant promise along in the way He planned. Through the birth of Abraham's son Isaac, God was laying the groundwork to show He was the One who could bring life from death. And today we know God has raised His own Son, Jesus, from the dead! The more well acquainted we become with Abraham's story, Jesus' resurrection can resonate with us in new ways – as an echo of a previous miracle in God's rescue plan.

Through Isaac, God brought life from an empty womb.
Through Jesus, God brought life from a sealed tomb.

And as God continued His covenant plan through Abraham, He also did not forget Hagar or Ishmael. They were made in His image just as Sarah, Abraham and Isaac were. God continued to care for them because He is good, and His favor and blessing depend on Him, not us.

Lord, thank You for the covenant promises You have been *faithful* to fulfill. Because You are near, we have every *good* thing — and we are truly *blessed*. We are so thankful for Your *patience* and Your *goodness* to all of Your people. Pour Your *patience* and *goodness* into us as we go about our days so that we can give others a small glimpse of Your character. In Jesus' name, *amen*.

NOTES

NOTES

WEEK
Four

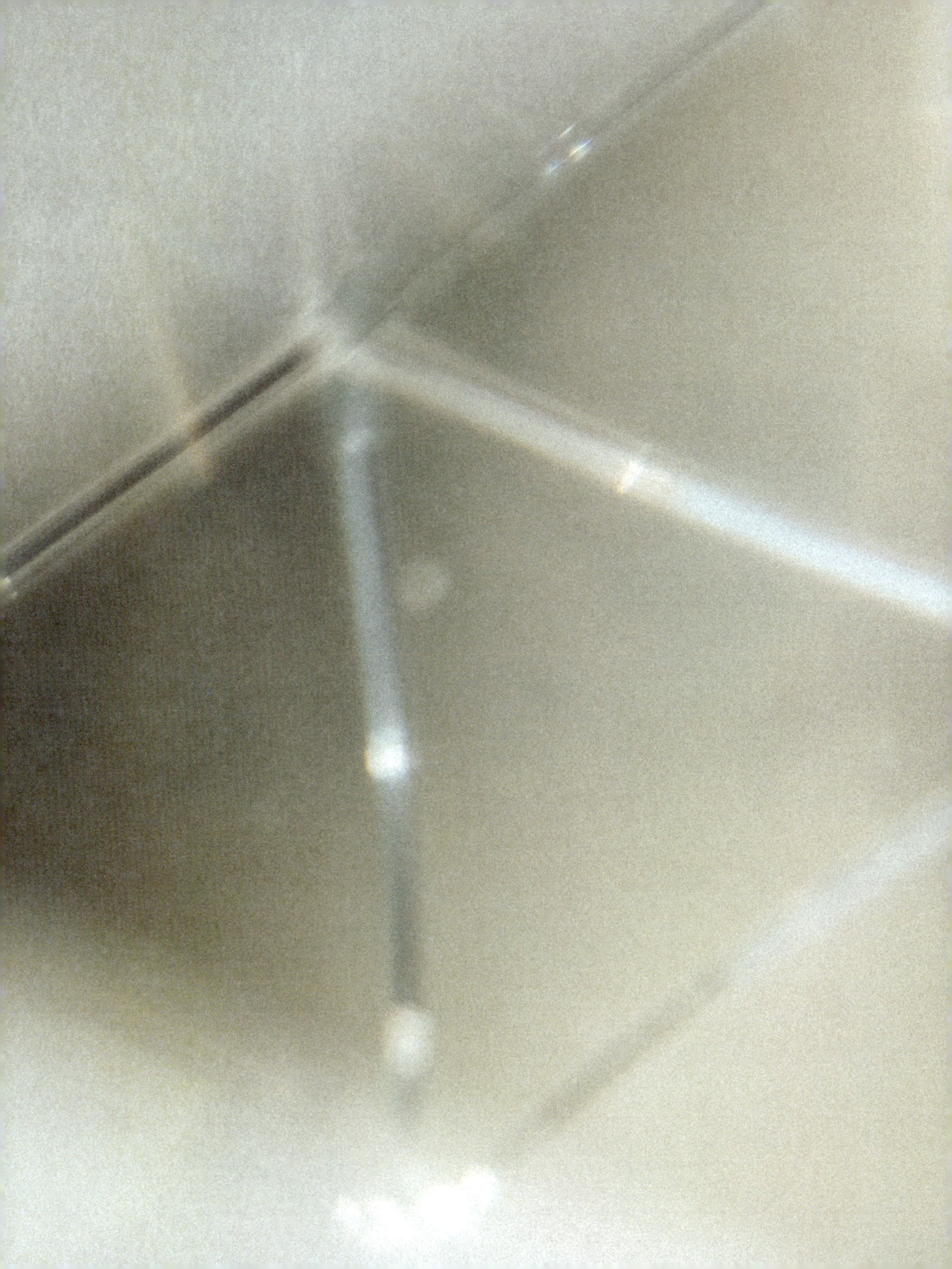

Day 16 - GENESIS **18-19**
The sinful cities of Sodom and Gomorrah faced divine judgment.

Editor's Note: *This lesson contains sensitive material. To those who have experienced sexual trauma or are triggered by reading texts that discuss sexual trauma, please proceed carefully.*

Last week, our study of Genesis ended with a sign of God's continued covenant with Abraham. This week, we will see how God continued to bless and teach Abraham, specifically teaching about His justice. Some lessons were hard for Abraham to grasp, but they were important — and we can learn from them too.

To start today's reading, Genesis 18:1 says *"the Lord appeared"* when three visitors arrived at Abraham's tent. When Abraham saw the three men, he welcomed them lavishly.
- Look over Abraham and Sarah's actions toward the visitors in Genesis 18:2-8, and write a few examples of how they showed hospitality. (This will be important later in today's study.)

In Genesis 18:10-14, God promised Abraham a son again, clearly specifying Sarah would be the mother. Sarah laughed. Maybe she was delighted at the absurdity of new life in her old age, or maybe she chuckled a bit skeptically — either way, God would keep His promise and fulfill His plans.

And God also had plans for the cities of Sodom and Gomorrah; as the three men walked with Abraham toward Sodom, Genesis 18:17-19 gives us a glimpse into His intentions.
- According to verse 19, why did God involve Abraham in what He was about to do? What was He teaching Abraham?

The unfolding story was designed for Abraham, a man of faith and a covenant partner with God, to learn about God's way of righteousness and justice. God had heard that "*the outcry against Sodom and Gomorrah [was] great and their sin [was] very grave*" (Genesis 18:20), but He was not capricious in measuring out justice. He wanted Abraham to know He double-checked (so to speak) and discerned the truth of the situation.

- Abraham asked God to consider saving the cities if there were righteous people living there: "*Suppose there are fifty righteous ...*" (Genesis 18:24). How many times in verses 25-32 did Abraham negotiate for a lower number? What does this reveal about Abraham's character, and what does it reveal about God's character that He engaged in this conversation?

Abraham was entering into his prophetic role as a blessing for the nations by interceding (praying, advocating) for the righteous. It may seem Abraham was changing God's mind about the fate of the cities, but God was teaching Abraham. One scholar describes their interaction as a "'philosophical discussion' ... more likely than 'negotiation session.'"[1] By allowing Abraham to push for mercy until he was satisfied, God revealed that Abraham could not outdo His mercy. Indeed, God ultimately saved the three people who were willing to leave the city.

- When have you been tempted to think you are more merciful than God? How does this exchange between Abraham and God teach you about His mercy?

The people of Sodom and Gomorrah were living in truly terrible sin. Against the backdrop of how Abraham welcomed strangers in Genesis 18, the inhospitality in Sodom and Gomorrah is glaring in Genesis 19. And the people were more than just unwelcoming: Genesis 19:4-9 describes threats of sexual assault. All recorded cultures of the ANE outlawed the crimes threatened here.[2] Most importantly, God forbids such evil (e.g., Deuteronomy 22:25).

No wonder pleas from these cities reached heaven! The Lord destroyed them, with Lot and his daughters barely escaping (Genesis 19:27-29).

- After his experience with the Lord, Abraham had a unique understanding about what happened in Sodom and Gomorrah and why. How does this story impact your own perspective of God's justice and righteousness?

The behavior of Sodom and Gomorrah was abhorrent, as was the behavior of Lot and his daughters in Genesis 19:30-38. Lot's daughters repeated some of the broken patterns they likely learned in Sodom. While the Bible *describes* these acts, that doesn't mean God *prescribes* (or approves of) what took place. Scripture always presents such instances of inappropriate sexual activity with the assumption that they are wicked. To know what God considers a healthy sexual relationship, we can always refer to His good design in Genesis 2:24-25.

As we wrap up today's study, it's undeniable this section of Scripture is difficult. It may be especially difficult if you or someone you love has experienced sexual trauma, and if so, please hear these words of comfort: God grieves with you, and there is healing in Him. Just as God dealt with Sodom and Gomorrah, He will ultimately deal with all sin, including the hurts perpetrated against us. He witnesses it all, He is merciful, and He Himself is justice and righteousness.

SEXUAL SIN AND ASSAULT IN GENESIS

In God's good order, sex is intended to be an intimate and safe experience between one husband and one wife (Genesis 2:24-25). But after Adam and Eve chose to exit God's order, sexual sin entered the human story.

Genesis doesn't shy away from this reality. It includes accounts like that of Sodom and Gomorrah to demonstrate the depths of human depravity. And anywhere Scripture records acts of sexual sin (like we see in Genesis 19), they are placed alongside other wicked behaviors to show they are not acceptable to God.

Sometimes our own profound wounding may make it hard to read Bible stories where people were in vulnerable situations, like Hagar, Lot's daughters, or (as we'll soon read) Dinah or Tamar. But Scripture never shames or blames survivors of sexual trauma because of their pasts or how others took advantage of them. God treats all people as made in His image (Genesis 1:26-27), and His Word portrays survivors who triumphed over their circumstances and who God treated with dignity and honor.

- Hagar, an enslaved Egyptian woman who bore Abraham's first son but was expelled from his family, uniquely encountered God and said, *"I have seen him who looks after me"* (Genesis 16:33).
- Tamar was abandoned by her husband's family and felt forced to prostitute herself to her father-in-law. (In biblical times, prostitution was often an occupation of survival.) Yet she is the first woman called *"righteous"* in the Bible (Genesis 38:26).
- Rahab was a Canaanite prostitute, but she was commended for her faith because she hid Israelite spies (Hebrews 11:31).
- Bathsheba suffered because of a king's lust (2 Samuel 11), but she ultimately had the honor of being in Jesus' lineage — along with Rahab and Tamar (Matthew 1:1-6).

Jesus, God Himself in the form of a man, best modeled how women and all people should be treated. He entered this world gently and humbly (Luke 2:1-21; Philippians 2:7). He persuaded people with stories (Luke 10:25-37) and shrugged off power plays (Luke 4:1-13). He traveled with women (Luke 8:1-3) and had theological conversations with them (John 4:1-26). Jesus healed women (Luke 8:43-48), defended them (John 8:1-11), and entrusted them with proclaiming the resurrection (Matthew 28). In Jesus' life, we see examples of godly, healthy interactions between men and women.

To sum up our Bible passages: Sexual sin causes brokenness and pain. Thankfully, though, God redeems.

"For he has not ignored or belittled the suffering of the needy. He has not turned his back on them, but has listened to their cries for help" (Psalm 22:24, NLT).

God listens. He never ignores or belittles those who are needy and suffering. God never turns His back on those who have been abused or those who feel broken.

He is the One we cling to when we read painful and traumatic stories in the Bible. And we cry out to Him when our own suffering feels like a valley of despair — we can take our pain to God, and He will hear us. Giving voice to these events and to our wounds can allow us to experience the miracle of God's healing and comfort. In other acts of great love, God also gives wisdom and insight (Proverbs 20:15; Proverbs 16:16; James 3:17-18) to professional counselors who can walk alongside us in our healing journey.

Dear friend, you are valuable and important, a woman made in the image of God, a person He loves. May God's comfort show you the way to peace and restoration.

Day 17 - GENESIS **20**

Abraham navigated challenges with Abimelech.

Wait ... Didn't we read this story already?

After reading Genesis 12, Genesis 20 feels a bit like déjà vu! Unfortunately, both stories have similar trajectories. Again, Abraham claimed Sarah was his sister, and again, Sarah was taken into the household of a king (Genesis 20:2). We might hope Abraham would behave differently this time than he did in Chapter 12 ... but he didn't. Abraham was flawed, just as we are, and was slow to learn this particular lesson.
- What is a lesson you have been slow to learn from God? How has He shown patience with you and given you second chances and fresh starts despite your mistakes?

Genesis 20 is similar to Genesis 12, but a few things did change between this episode and the last one.
- Compare the stories by filling in the blank sections of this chart:

	GENESIS 12:10-20	GENESIS 20
Who was king?	Pharaoh	Abimelech
Who revealed that Sarah was Abraham's wife?	Unknown	
How did the king get rid of the sickness in his household?	Presumably by sending Abram and Sarai away with all their property	

- What was Abraham's perception of the relationship between God and Abimelech's people in Genesis 20:11? Was Abraham's perception right?

85

God communicated directly to Abimelech in Genesis 20:3, and just like Pharaoh, Abimelech wanted to fix the problem immediately. Abimelech *did* have a fear of God and *did not* want to be accused of adultery. This town and the people in it seem to have been very different from Sodom and Gomorrah, where the people were so unwilling to fear God that angels nearly had to drag Lot and his daughters to safety (Genesis 19:16).

So it seems Abraham had more to learn about God's mercy toward people.
- In Genesis 18:23 and Genesis 20:4, Abimelech and Abraham both asked God a similar question. What did they ask? How did God respond?

Abraham was the first named prophet in the Old Testament (Genesis 20:7), and a prophet's job was to act as a mediator between people and God, almost always dealing with ethical concerns. This time, Abraham was asked to intercede on behalf of a king whom he had misunderstood and whom he had nearly caused to commit adultery.

Specifically, Abimelech needed Abraham to pray for God to heal him and his household because his family was barren (Genesis 20:17-18). Abraham's prayer for Abimelech may have been similar to what he had prayed for his own household many times as he and Sarah walked through infertility (Genesis 11:30). It likely felt like a well-traveled road.
- When have you repeatedly prayed for something for yourself or for others? How has your prayer changed or remained the same over the years? When you feel discouraged by an apparent lack of reply from God, how do you find motivation to keep praying?

Today's scriptures show us God was shaping Abraham to think about the nations through *God's lens* rather than his own. When Abraham thought he needed to plead for the righteous in Sodom and Gomorrah, God surprised him by revealing He was already well aware. When Abraham thought there was not a God-fearing leader in Gerar, God surprised him again, showing him there was. And then God used Abraham's well-practiced pleas for children on behalf of that very leader, whom Abraham had hurt.
- Do you feel open to God's surprises? Prayerfully ask for God's help to trust Him fully and to live with expectation for things you can't see yet.

Day 18 – GENESIS **21**

Isaac was born, and Hagar and Ishmael were sent away.

The long-awaited day arrived! God blessed Abraham and Sarah with a son, Isaac. It's easy to imagine they laughed with delight every time they said his name (which means "he laughs" in Hebrew).

Unfortunately, the tension between Sarah and Hagar continued. One day Sarah saw Hagar's son, Ishmael (probably around 7 years old), laughing unkindly at Isaac (probably around 3 years old). Sarah's inner "mama bear," and perhaps some insecurities, awoke — she told Abraham that she'd had enough and that Hagar and Ishmael must leave (Genesis 21:9-10).

This was an awful and broken solution to an awful and broken problem. Sarah, Abraham and Hagar were at an impasse. All their problem-solving methods were based on their own idea of what was right. The text does not indicate whether God was displeased, but we know He was able to protect Hagar and Ishmael regardless of where they lived, and He allowed Sarah's plan to go forward (vv. 12-14).

As a result, we have the first single mom in the Bible.

Hagar and her son weren't part of the family line God chose and called to carry out His covenant promise to Abraham. She was booted out by God's people, alone and without resources. It would be easy to understand if she doubted whether God could see her or hear her anymore.
- Maybe some of Hagar's story sounds familiar to you. When have you been pushed out or treated as less-than? On the other hand, when have you treated other people unkindly? How does this allow you to relate to today's scriptures?

We all know what it feels like to walk around with broken instincts in broken circumstances. So this is an important part of the story to lean into: Let's see how God treated the first abandoned child and the first single mom in Scripture.
- Read Genesis 21:15-18. Who did God hear?

God was still paying attention to Hagar and Ishmael. No, they weren't a part of God's plan for Abraham, but *they were a part of God's plan*. The rest of their story may not be noted in the biblical narrative, but they did not disappear from God's notice.

- In her time of need, the God who saw Hagar opened her eyes so she could see the solution she had missed in her grief. What did she see in Genesis 21:19?

- According to verse 20, who was God "*with*" in the wilderness?

The first fatherless child in Scripture was cared for by the Creator of the universe. Later in the Bible, God repeatedly instructed His people to care for widows, orphans and foreigners (Deuteronomy 24:17-19; Isaiah 1:17; Zechariah 7:9-10; James 1:27; etc.). But first, God demonstrated that He Himself cares for those in vulnerable situations. In Genesis, He did the "show" before the "tell."

Just as God saw the broken situations and broken instincts in Hagar and Ishmael's story, He saw the brokenness in Abraham's story and would continue to see all things in the coming stories in Genesis. This same God sees all of us today.

- What situations and instincts feel broken in your life? How might you be tempted to react wrongly because of wrongs done to you? How does being seen by God change your outlook and reactions?

- As you meditate on how God *saw* His people in Genesis, what are some ways you can *see* others around you? Ask God to show you people who are hurting or who may feel left out, and brainstorm some ways to acknowledge or help them.

Day 19 – GENESIS 22
Abraham was tested.

Today's Genesis story can be hard for us to read and understand, in part because it is set firmly in ANE culture and customs. Child sacrifice, which is referenced in Genesis 22, was a culturally understood concept in the ANE, but it's easy for us to get lost in the foreign details and miss the plot. Fortunately, God clearly explained what was happening from His perspective, which helps us not to get lost in ours.

- Read Genesis 22:1-2. What was God doing?

- To read why God was doing this, we will skip ahead to Genesis 22:12b. What did God want to "*know*"?

Thus far in Genesis, God had revealed to Abraham that He is a God of generosity, blessing, mercy, justice and righteousness. Through Abraham's acts of faith and failure, God had proven faithful. Their relationship spanned years and miles. Now, God wanted to know if Abraham valued the gifts more than the Giver.

Scripture testifies that God is omniscient, meaning He has all understanding of all things (Romans 11:33-36), including the depths of every human heart (John 2:25; Psalm 139:1-3). But it seems He wanted to test Abraham to reveal to him the desires of his own heart.

- What do 1 Peter 1:7 and James 1:3-4 say about the purpose of testing? How might this help us understand Genesis 22?

In all of God's past requests of Abraham, He included a promised blessing. In Genesis 22:2, there was only a request: *"Take your son, your only son Isaac, whom you love, and go to the land of Moriah, and offer him there ..."* Instead of reiterating a promise or expanding one, God called Abraham to rely on His goodness and faithfulness to keep His promise that Isaac would carry the covenant forward.

Back in Genesis 3:5-6, Adam and Eve wondered if God was keeping blessings from them, and they chose to disobey and seek autonomy. This wasn't like a mischievous child harmlessly sneaking a treat from the kitchen. Their disobedience directly stemmed from a lack of trust in God's revealed character, disordering God's perfect order.

Now Abraham faced a similar choice: Did he trust God's character and believe God would somehow keep His promises through Isaac, even if Isaac died (Hebrews 11:17-19)? Or would Abraham decide his love for Isaac superseded his love for God? Would Abraham stay within God's good order?

- Read Genesis 22:9-13, and describe what happened:

Child sacrifice was a known form of pagan worship in the ANE, and for people at this time, it would have been unsurprising to think a deity would ask for a portion of a provided blessing, such as crops — or in this case, Isaac.[1] Later, God would explicitly outlaw child sacrifice (Leviticus 18:21; Deuteronomy 12:31). But when God stopped Abraham from sacrificing Isaac, it would have been surprising to the surrounding cultures, proving God does not desire or delight in the death of a child.
- God then emphasized and expanded on His covenant promise after Abraham obeyed. Read Genesis 22:15-18, and note any additional blessings in comparison to Genesis 12:1-3, Genesis 15:5 and Genesis 17:4-8.

When we look at our blessings, we often think we know the best plans for them. This includes our skills, talents, money, family, job, car ... really anything God has given us. We easily shift from *enjoying* God's gifts to *depending* on them for our joy or satisfaction. It's a thin line. Ultimately, though, being overly attached to earthly blessings is disordered and leads us to think and act in ways that don't reflect God's character.

God delights in giving good gifts and is eager to bless. He also is a God of good order.
- What gifts give you deep joy or satisfaction? Pray that God would help you to rightly enjoy the gifts He has given but to order them under your worship of Him as the Giver (James 1:17).

Day 20 – GENESIS 23-24

Rebekah's story unfolded.

So far in Genesis, we've gotten to know Sarah and Abraham well throughout their journey with God; however, today's scriptures begin with the end of Sarah's life. After grieving, Abraham purchased a piece of land for her burial rites.

- Where did Abraham purchase property, according to Genesis 23:19-20 (specifically, what "*land*" was it in)? How does this relate to Genesis 17:8?

- How much did the land cost, and why do you think he insisted on paying, according to Genesis 23:10-16?

This purchase was an act of faith. Abraham knew this land would eventually belong to his family because it was in Canaan, the promised land, so he paid the very expensive price without haggling.

Upon Sarah's death, Abraham also realized his son Isaac needed a wife. He and Isaac wanted to ensure God's covenant promise would continue through their family, but they lived far away from anyone Isaac could marry. Somehow, they had to find a wife from Abraham's hometown who was also willing to leave her home and travel far away because Isaac needed to live in the promised land.

- Abraham sent his servant to search for a wife for Isaac. How would the servant choose the right wife, according to Genesis 24:10-14?

It's important to note this is another passage of Scripture that is descriptive, not prescriptive; this story describes how the servant found Rebekah as a wife for Isaac, but it's not a story telling us how to find God's will or our own spouse!

ANE readers of Genesis would have recognized that the servant was seeking an oracle. This ancient practice involved offering up a question to a god (for example, *Should I marry him?*) and specifying the way the answer should come (for example, *If the harvest is good, it's a "yes"*). Oracles are troublesome because they put humanity in the driver's seat, trying to force God to answer. Attempting to back God into a corner is never a good idea (Deuteronomy 6:16; Romans 11:33-35). God sometimes worked with

oracles, as in Genesis 24, but such stories usually indicate spiritual immaturity on the part of those who asked God for a sign (see also Judges 6:36-40 and 1 Samuel 6:8-12).
- This is not to say God is reluctant to communicate. God communicated a lot in Genesis! Starting with the verses below, look back over the weeks you've completed in this study, and note some examples of who God communicated with, when and how.

    - Genesis 4:6-10:

    - Genesis 7:1:

    - Genesis 16:8-10:

    -

    -

    -

In the ancient world, most people did not expect their primary deity to speak to common people. Instead, people would seek out priests, who would elicit omens, interpret dreams or the innards of animals, or read "signs" from the gods in the sky. But from the beginning, the one true God has spoken clearly to His people when He wants to say something. No secret formulas, no need for perfect words — just God and people simply speaking.
- Have you ever felt unqualified to talk to God? Have you ever thought a pastor or ministry leader had better access to God than you do? After learning that God has always reached down to common people to converse with them, how does this encourage you to pray boldly and know you are heard?

- Many of us have prayed for an oracle at some point. (For example: *God, please make it sunny tomorrow if I'll get a promotion — but if it's rainy, I'll stay at this level forever.*) As you learn to trust God's character, how can you pray and make decisions knowing that you are made in His image, valuable and purposed to reflect Him?

WEEK **FOUR**
Reflection

Abraham had quite a journey — both literally and figuratively. From leading a not-so-noteworthy life in Ur to making a covenant with the almighty God, Abraham's highs and lows were extraordinary. This week, we read how Abraham learned about God's righteousness and justice at Sodom and Gomorrah, discovered upright leaders in Canaanite cities, and passed God's test to see if he feared Him.

After Adam and Noah, Abraham was the first patriarch of the nation of Israel, and Genesis tells his story with all its ups and downs. His journey sets the tone not for how humanity is supposed to behave but for how *God behaves* even when we fail. The path Abraham took should give us great hope because it reveals a God who will stay with us and finish whatever He starts.

As Abraham's story was ending, Isaac's story continued, and he found a wife from his father's hometown. Rebekah left her home quickly (Genesis 24:58), which may even remind us of Abraham's earlier obedience when God called him to leave home (Genesis 12:1-4). Next week, we'll see how the covenant relationship between God and His people continued as Isaac took his place as the head of the family.

Would Isaac struggle as his father had? Would he be able to pass on the covenant? Was Abraham special somehow, such that God would remove His promise if Isaac didn't measure up? These are all questions the author of Genesis wants us to think about.

We will never fully understand God's ways. He is a mystery unfathomable to us. But we can always rely on His character, revealed in the gospel, because it is the most constant thing in this ever-changing universe. Genesis illustrates God's goodness from the beginning and invites us into the whole story. The actions of God were likely befuddling to Abraham and others, too, but we have the privilege of a backstage view. We get to see the ways God's character is consistent even when His ways are mysterious.

Lord, please guide us as we walk with You. Help us to follow in Your steps, being *obedient* to Your call. Thank You for the example of Abraham and for Your *faithfulness* through generations. We want to *love* You more, *know* You more and *trust* You more. May Your mysterious ways *encourage* us to rely on Your consistent character. In Jesus' name, *amen*.

NOTES

NOTES

WEEK
Five

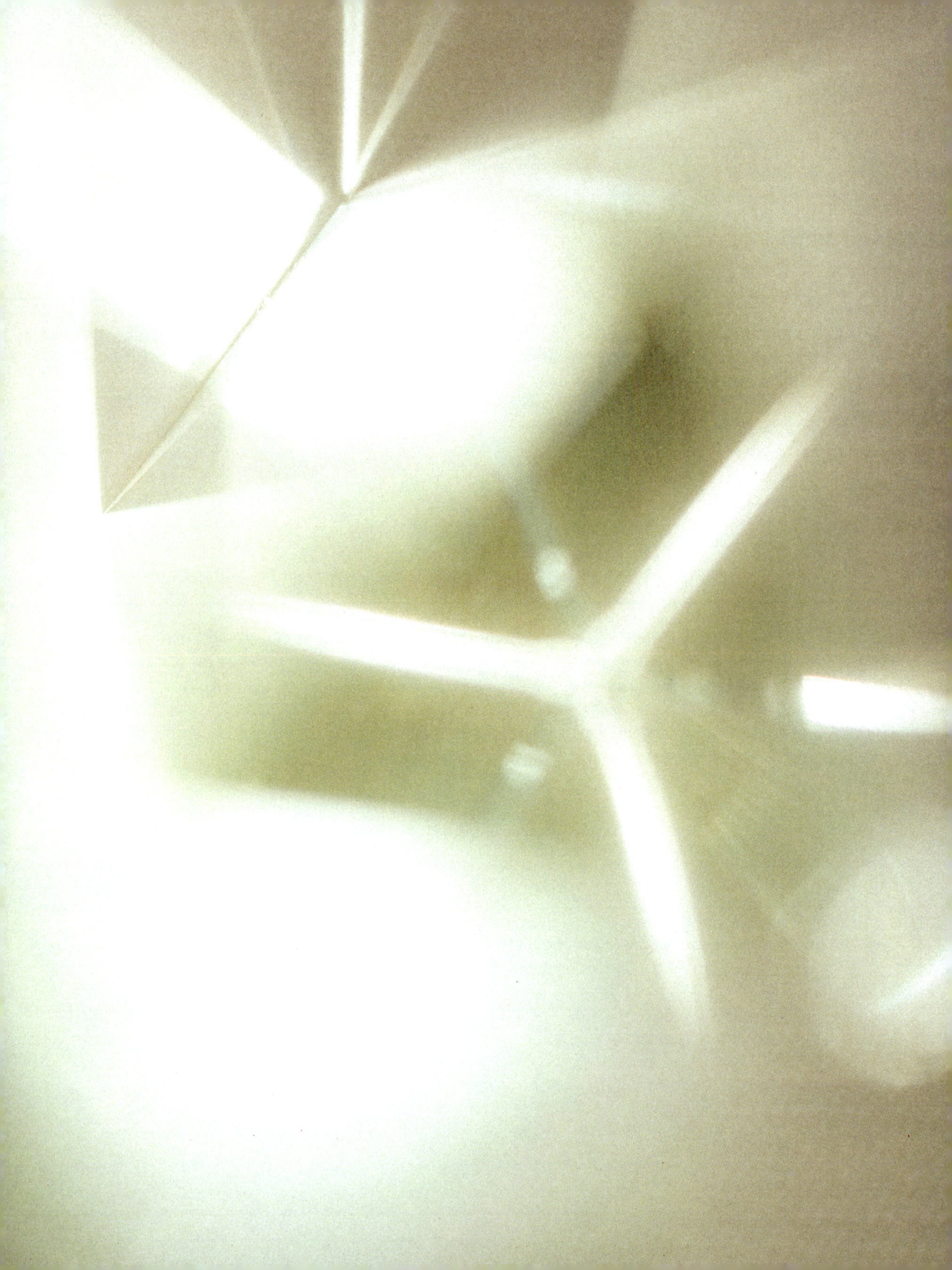

Day 21 - GENESIS 25-26:33

Jacob and Esau would become two nations, and Esau sold his birthright.

In today's reading, Abraham's story on earth came to a close (Genesis 25:8); he lived a long life and died surrounded by family. His sons Isaac and Ishmael buried him with Sarah. Even though Isaac carried the covenant blessing, God also took care of Ishmael as well as Abraham's other family members, and Ishmael's family was recorded in Genesis 25:12-18.

After Abraham died, Isaac's story formally began with his own genealogy. Though it's only described in one verse (Genesis 25:21), we also see that Isaac and Rebekah struggled with barrenness for 20 years (vv. 20, 26b) before the Lord enabled them to conceive twins.

- While carrying the twins, Rebekah asked God about the jostling going on in her. What did He tell her in Genesis 25:23?

- What did they name the boys in verses 25-26?

In the ANE it was not uncommon to name a child after the circumstances of their birth. In Hebrew, Jacob's name meant "may God protect," but it also sounded like the word for "heel" (as well as a word meaning "deceiver" or "cheater," which will come into play later in the story).[1] Esau was named for his appearance, as "Esau" meant "red" or "hairy."[2]

- The boys were very different! Write down the descriptors of Esau and Isaac in Genesis 25:27-28. How did their parents respond to them differently?

Favoritism never yields good fruit (Proverbs 28:21; James 2:9). The seeds of division planted between the brothers grew, and eventually Jacob tried to put himself between Esau and the family birthright. Jacob held a bowl of stew over a hungry Esau's head in Genesis 25:29-34 and said, *"Sell me your birthright now."*

- Jacob certainly wasn't kind, but Genesis condemns Esau here. How did Esau treat his birthright, according to Genesis 25:34?

A birthright was the allotment of everything one's father had. In the ANE, the firstborn son generally received a double portion (Deuteronomy 21:17). Isaac had two sons, so the inheritance would have been divided into three segments, with the oldest (Esau) receiving two of the three portions. When Esau so quickly gave up this enormous gift, he was treating a great honor as if it were nothing.

- Just as Eve "*saw … desired … took … and ate*" with a quick succession of verbs in Genesis 3:6, how does Genesis 25:34 show a similar pattern with Esau? What do we learn from this echo of Eden?

After a famine hit the land, Isaac and his family settled in Gerar (which was in Canaan, as you can see on the map on Page 54). God told him to stay in the promised land.

- We learn more about Isaac's time in Gerar in Genesis 26:6-23, but for the purposes of our study, let's focus on the promises that bookend this chapter. What did God promise to Isaac in Genesis 26:3-5 and verse 24?

Isaac stayed in Gerar and reestablished wells his father had dug. He planted, harvested and became wealthy. He was growing roots in the land God had promised his family.

Some people recognized Isaac was blessed and either envied him, asked him to leave or feared him — but those who were afraid made a covenant of peace with him (Genesis 26:28-29). Though it didn't always lead to favor among men, God's hand in Isaac's life was unmistakable.

- In Genesis 26:28, Abimelech and others told Isaac, "*We see plainly that the Lord has been with you.*" How do you "*see plainly*" God's faithfulness in Isaac's story so far? How do you see His faithfulness in your own story?

Day 22 – GENESIS **26:34-28:9**

Jacob stole Esau's blessing.

In the Old Testament, God gave His people commands against marrying foreigners, or people outside of the Israelite nation (Exodus 34:16; Deuteronomy 7:3; 1 Kings 11:2). These commands weren't about race but rather about faith: God didn't want for His people to unite themselves with nonbelievers or for pagan parents to teach their children a false religion they were raised in. (And we see in 2 Corinthians 6:14 a similar principle for believers today.)

> **Could non-Israelites join God's covenant community in the Old Testament?**
> *We know God regarded marriage between Israelites and non-Israelites as a faith issue, not a social one, because foreigners were always welcome to enter Israel and embrace God as their God (Leviticus 19:33-34; Deuteronomy 10:18-19). In Exodus, when God saved His people from slavery in Egypt, many outside of Israel's family joined them (Exodus 12:38). When the Israelites crossed into the promised land, a Canaanite prostitute named Rahab helped them (Joshua 2-6), then married an Israelite man, and ultimately became part of Christ's genealogy (Ruth 4:21; Matthew 1:5). Her son, Boaz, married a faithful Moabite woman named Ruth, who is also in Christ's genealogy (Matthew 1:5). God made His covenant promise to Israel (Abraham's family) because, as a testimony of His faithfulness, He would send our Savior through this family. That didn't mean it was a closed group, though. As Rahab and Ruth prove, anyone was invited to participate in the community and embrace God as their God.*

But Genesis 26:34-35 took place before God formally gave His law — so perhaps Isaac didn't insist that Esau find a wife from his family (as Abraham had found for Isaac and as Isaac would later find for Jacob). Or perhaps Esau went against Isaac's wishes, but either way, he married two Hittite women, who would have worshipped false gods.

Isaac's family was strained and breaking.

And this continued in Genesis 27. As Jacob had taken advantage of Esau's hunger to steal his birthright, now Rebekah and Jacob plotted to take advantage of Isaac's blindness to steal his blessing.

- Disguised as Esau, Jacob "*went in to his father*" (Genesis 27:18). Isaac asked multiple questions to verify his son's identity. Read Genesis 27:18-25, and write down Jacob's answers:

Isaac's Question or Statement	Jacob's Response
"Who are you, my son?" (v. 18c).	(v. 19).
"How is it that you have found [this food] so quickly, my son?" (v. 20).	(v. 20).
"Please come near, that I may feel you ..." (v. 21).	Jacob realized he had spoken too much.
"The voice is Jacob's voice ..." (v. 22).	
"Are you really my son Esau?" (v. 24a)	(v. 24b).

In the end, Jacob received the blessing. But at what cost?
- Both Isaac and Esau had intense reactions when they realized what had happened. How did Isaac react in Genesis 27:33? What about Esau in verses 34, 38 and 41?

- When Rebekah discovered Esau's desire to kill Jacob, what did she tell Jacob to do in Genesis 27:42-45?

- Which of the above responses do you tend toward in broken situations? (Do you tend toward anger, fear, resentment, trying to "fix" things, etc.?) What might it look like to submit to the Lord in such moments of intense emotion?

Rebekah didn't want to lose both her sons on the same day, but in a sense, she may have. Through favoritism and deceit, she undermined her relationship with Esau. That same deceit resulted in Jacob fleeing for his life. He likely never saw her again. (Scripture doesn't mention Rebekah at the reunion of Esau and Jacob in Genesis 33:4-12 nor at the death of Isaac in Genesis 35:29, which may suggest she herself had already passed away.)

Between Esau's treatment of his birthright and Jacob's trickery, neither son seemed like a good fit to carry on the covenant. Nevertheless, Isaac passed on the covenant blessing to Jacob (Genesis 28:3-4). Jacob was a deceiver who took advantage of weakness for his own gain — but God still chose him and would use him to bless the whole world, just as He had chosen Abraham and Isaac despite their faults.

God is always looking for a way to bless people. It's who He is and how He leans. Our obvious flaws and deeply entrenched issues do not deter Him.
- We haven't gotten to this verse in our study yet, but look up Genesis 50:20. What does God do with evil human plans?

Jacob's story showcases God's goodness, mercy, patience and faithfulness. Jacob was a sinful person just like you and me, and throughout his whole life (spoiler alert!), he struggled with the same temptations and tendencies, grasping at gain and looking out for himself. But even this points us to the God who is working toward redemption for sinners! His messed-up people could not mess up His plan. Abraham, Isaac and Jacob belonged to God, but they were not the heroes: God was.
- How has God been a hero in your story? Ask Him to show you ways He has brought about redemption in your life or the lives of those you love. As you pray, consider creative ways to express your thanks! (Some ideas: Write a few words of thanks in your Bible, decorate a small notecard with a scripture of gratitude, play a worship song and praise God, paint or draw a picture that represents what you're thankful for, etc.)

Day 23 - GENESIS 28:10-22
God restated to Jacob the covenant He had started with Abram.

In yesterday's scriptures, Jacob fled for his life. Even though he left his parents on relatively good terms, his brother Esau was threatening to murder him — so Jacob was in a vulnerable spot in today's passage. Stopping for the night, he finally lay down to sleep with a rock for a pillow.
- What did Jacob dream about in Genesis 28:12-15? Does it surprise you that God gave this dream to someone who had just stolen a blessing, deceived and divided his family, and run from the consequences? Why or why not?

In the ancient world, many people thought gods used stairs to travel from heaven to earth.[1] The ladder in Jacob's dream may seem a little unusual to us, but it would have fit into his understanding of how God worked.

And God spoke to Jacob, confirming that, as Isaac had said, Jacob would indeed carry the covenant forward through his family. Jacob would receive the land and the many offspring initially promised to Abraham.

God also added something unique to His promise to Jacob: With the backdrop of angels doing His bidding, moving from heaven to earth, God promised Jacob He would be **with him.** *"Behold, I am with you and will keep you wherever you go ... I will not leave you ..."* (v. 15). Jacob is the first person in Scripture to whom God made this promise with the words *"I will not leave you."*
- Why do you think God assured Jacob of His presence and protection at this particular time in his life?

Jacob was about 60 miles into a 550-mile journey.[2] Alone, afraid and perhaps remorseful, Jacob was neck-deep in the consequences of his actions. *This* is where God met Jacob and offered him blessing and protection.

- Identify a time in your life when you have experienced consequences of your own unwise choices. How have you seen God bless and protect you or lead you out of a situation you thought couldn't possibly get better? How does this help you trust that despite your mistakes, God will continue to carry you forward?

When he woke up, Jacob's response was to build an altar and worship. The very rock he had used as a pillow became the foundation for the altar.
- Jacob also said a vow to God, using an if/then formula that was common in the ANE. In Genesis 28:20-22, Jacob said, *"If God will be with me ..."* then what would happen?

Jacob's response to God's promise was to bargain. In a sense, he said *if* God was faithful to him, Jacob would *then* be faithful to God. Essentially he said, "We'll see when I get back." His position wasn't commendable, but neither did God chastise him. God partnered in covenant with Jacob and met him where he was. Just as God picked Abraham, He picked unruly Jacob.

Jacob's bold bargaining may surprise us, but it ultimately shows us that God's faithfulness does not rest on our level of faith. Genesis also holds up Jacob's lack of faith and asks us if we see anything familiar. Are we fickle, or are we steadfast? Are we quick to doubt, or are we eager to believe? Do we ask God only for more power and more stuff, or do we ask for more faith and more strength?
- Recall some times you, like Jacob, have been a little unruly with God. Before God, how can you humbly recognize those times of stubbornness while also remembering He delights in His children and gives us time to grow in faith? Thanking God for His faithfulness, patience and kindness, let's ask for more faith and walk with assurance that He will provide it (Luke 17:5).

Day 24 – GENESIS **29-30**

Jacob married Laban's daughters and had children, and his flocks increased.

After months of traveling, Jacob arrived at his uncle Laban's home in the region of modern-day Turkey and Syria. Jacob's instant attraction to Rachel and his willingness to pay an oversized bride price (which was customary in the ANE) made for a romantic start to their story.[1] Though Jacob agreed to seven years of work for Laban, it seemed like *"but a few days because of the love he had for her"* (Genesis 29:20b).

The fresh start turned sour, however, when Laban tricked Jacob by secretly exchanging Rachel for his other daughter, Leah, during the marriage ceremony (Genesis 29:22-25). Now Jacob, who had previously taken advantage of his brother and father in their weakness, was taken advantage of by his uncle. The tables turned, and this time, the deceiver was deceived.

Especially since he didn't have other family members nearby, Jacob had no recourse and was forced to follow Laban's new stipulations to work for another seven years to marry Rachel (Genesis 29:27-28). There is much we can learn from Rachel and Leah themselves and from their relationship as sisters and women – but for today, let's look at the names of their children. These names were a testimony to the tumultuous household atmosphere.

- Take a look at the chart titled "Jacob's Sons Born in Paddan-aram" on Page 109. We can hear these children's names and the comments about them as back-and-forth between the sisters, a public spat for all to witness. Write down a few insights you glean from what Rachel and Leah said or felt as they named their children:

- According to Genesis 29:32-33, Leah felt seen and heard by God. What other woman in Genesis testified to the same thing? (Hint: Look back at Genesis 16:13.) How are their stories similar?

God continued to fulfill His promise to bless and increase, despite the drama along the way.

After Rachel gave birth to Joseph, and presumably after Jacob's years of working for Laban had passed, Jacob was ready to go back to his *"own home and country"* (Genesis 30:25). Jacob did not want to return empty-handed, so he proposed a bargain with Laban: Jacob would tend to a group of Laban's sheep and goats, and after they bred, Jacob would keep some of the offspring.
- Which goats and lambs would Jacob take from the flock, according to Genesis 30:32-33? Does this seem like a fair deal, or do you think Jacob was back to his trickster tendencies?

Jacob's request was actually very reasonable and likely much smaller than what he was entitled to.[2] Laban agreed to the deal.
- What did Jacob do with sticks in Genesis 30:37-43 to ensure a good, strong group of speckled goats and sheep? Did it work?

Jacob certainly thought the "magic sticks" were responsible for making him prosperous. Spoiler alert: They weren't. Still, it seems that for a time, God was content to let Jacob think he was the one who had outsmarted Laban.
- When have you experienced unusual favor and attributed it primarily to your own cleverness or efforts? Go ahead and chuckle a bit at yourself, and thank God for the gift of hindsight. Ask Him to help you develop *insight* to see where He is blessing you today and to praise Him for it in real time!

JACOB'S SONS BORN IN PADDAN-ARAM

CHILD'S PARENTS	CHILD'S NAME	NAME'S HEBREW MEANING	COMMENTARY FROM MOM
Jacob and Leah	Reuben	"He has seen my misery" or "see, a son."	"... The LORD has looked upon my affliction; for now my husband will love me" (Genesis 29:32).
Jacob and Leah	Simeon	"One who hears."	"... Because the LORD has heard that I am hated, he has given me this son also" (Genesis 29:33a).
Jacob and Leah	Levi	"Attached."	"... Now this time my husband will be attached to me ..." (Genesis 29:34).
Jacob and Leah	Judah	"Praise."	"... This time I will praise the LORD" (Genesis 29:35a).
Jacob and Bilhah (Rachel's servant)	Dan	"He has vindicated."	"... God has judged me, and has also heard my voice and given me a son" (Genesis 30:6a).
Jacob and Bilhah (Rachel's servant)	Naphtali	"My struggle."	"... With mighty wrestlings I have wrestled with my sister and have prevailed" (Genesis 30:8a).
Jacob and Zilpah (Leah's servant)	Gad	"Good fortune."	"... Good fortune has come!" (Genesis 30:11).
Jacob and Zilpah (Leah's servant)	Asher	"Happy."	"... Happy am I! For women have called me happy" (Genesis 30:13a-b).
Jacob and Leah	Issachar	"Reward."	"... God has given me my wages ..." (Genesis 30:18a).
Jacob and Leah	Zebulun	"Honor."	"... God has endowed me with a good endowment; now my husband will honor me ..." (Genesis 30:20a).
Jacob and Rachel	Joseph	"May he add."	"... God has taken away my reproach ... May the LORD add to me another son!" (Genesis 30:23-24).*

*God answered Rachel's prayer with Benjamin, the youngest and final son of Jacob. Benjamin was born later, however, and not in Paddan-aram (Genesis 35:17-18).

RESTORATION *After* REJECTION

From the moment we meet her in Genesis 29, we see Leah had it rough. Between her disappointed husband, her manipulative father, the cultural norms and expectations for women, and her "*eyes [that] were weak*" (Genesis 29:17), making her less culturally attractive than her younger sister ... Leah didn't have a lot of positive things going for her. How was she able to cope? This seems downright awful.

Some of us may feel extra empathy for Leah because we've experienced similar struggles. We didn't choose trauma, rejection, disappointment or illness, yet it found its way into our life. It may seem like we're only surviving, not thriving. After a traumatic childhood, exclusion when we wanted to belong, unhealthy relationships, failing health, or other hardships, we wonder if we're destined to be desperate forever.

A fresh start with a clean slate appears the only way out of our tangled mess. But whether we find ourselves sinking in consequences of our own choices or drowning in someone else's decisions, we may begin to wonder if God cares enough to pull us out and give us a fresh start.

Does He see? Does He hear? Does He care? Is this as good as it gets?

Friend, God is with us. Not only are we not alone, but it is God's character to see, hear and bless. He doesn't necessarily step into our broken environments and fix everything instantly, but He does find disorder and help us restore it. With the same creative power He used in creation, He speaks and provides, delighting in His image bearers every step of the way.

Leah's first three sons were named from her longing to be loved by Jacob (Genesis 29:32-34). But by the time her fourth son, Judah, was born, she put all that aside and simply said, "*This time I will praise the LORD*" (v. 35). Wouldn't you love to know what happened between her third and fourth sons? Somewhere in there, Leah let go of her need to be loved by Jacob, and she set her sights on the One who was able to meet her in the middle of a broken relationship.

It is in God's nature to see all our messes and lean in. He is looking for a way to bless, longing to work *with* us toward full restoration of our present issues and past wounds. The question isn't if God cares enough to help us. The question is: Are we willing to invite God into our messes and seek His restoration of what is broken? Will we live like people loved by God? Will we let Him into the hidden and hurting places in our hearts, trusting that whatever He reveals, He can heal?

It's hard work, this restoration business. But God will be with us on this difficult path, and many of His people throughout history can testify that the other side is more beautiful than we can imagine. By letting God into our wounds and inviting His Spirit to renew our minds (Romans 12:2), we get to watch the miracles He performs along the way. It is worth it.

Leah's son Judah struggled, but eventually his family and the family of Benjamin (Rachel's youngest son) made up the southern kingdom of Israel (1 Kings 12:20-21). From the tribe of Judah came Jesus (Matthew 1:2-3). So through Leah's family, God sent the Savior who would bless the entire world! God can and will redeem us from the rubble too.

Day 25 - GENESIS 31

Jacob ran from Laban.

Jacob's time living with his uncle came to an end when Laban's sons became frustrated and jealous of Jacob's success. Jacob knew it was time to leave, and the Lord confirmed that he needed to depart right away (Genesis 31:1-3).
- In Genesis 31:11-13, what did the angel of God tell Jacob about his livestock? Who was responsible for the speckled animals? (Look back at Genesis 30:31-39 if you need a refresher on why these animals were important!)

Though Jacob may have thought his sticks had made the animals speckled, God clarified *He was the One responsible for the blessing.* Then He told Jacob it was time to go, and Jacob made the choice to leave with his family and livestock in secret (Genesis 31:17-18). Laban's daughters felt cheated out of their inheritance, and Rachel seemed to feel justified in stealing *"her father's household gods"* in verse 19. These were likely small household idols for protection and fertility — notably, there were not related to worship of the one true God.[1]

Laban gave chase and caught up with Jacob's caravan. Before they had an epic showdown, the Lord stepped in and spoke to Laban in a dream.
- What did God tell Laban in Genesis 31:24?

The phrase rendered as *"either good or bad"* in the ESV Bible could also be translated "from good to bad." God was instructing Laban not to say something good that he would then *turn into* something bad (as Laban had done by deceiving Jacob previously: in Jacob's marriage to Rachel, when Laban changed Jacob's wages, etc.).[2] It was a warning against being duplicitous.

But pretty soon the buildup of 20 years of mistrust and frustrations bubbled over as Jacob and Laban had it out in a mighty confrontation.
- What were Laban's issues in Genesis 31:26-30? What were Jacob's arguments in verses 36-42?

Ultimately, Laban had no recourse against Jacob, and the two made a covenant. This covenant was not an agreement to develop a supportive relationship, but it was an agreement to move on in peace. With their "meal and deal," they declared, *"The Lord watch between you and me, when we are out of one another's sight"* (Genesis 31:49). This statement may sound sweet, but it was a reminder to be truthful because God was watching. The two tricksters were putting each other on notice. Then they set up a pillar, a "line in the sand" of sorts, promising not to cross it toward one another with harmful intent (vv. 51-52).

Sometimes, there isn't a clear path to peace. In our world, we can be tempted to seek revenge and "clap back" at every offense — or maybe we're tempted to "cancel" and sever ties harshly and irrevocably with people we dislike or disagree with, including those who have deeply harmed us. But there is wisdom in Jacob and Laban's agreement to cease fighting and not pursue one another's harm.

- What situations are you facing that may be best served by agreeing to disagree? How can you commit not to pursue the harm of those you disagree with, including in the way you think and speak about them moving forward? Ask God to show you how to model peace in your heart and habits.

WEEK **FIVE**
Reflection

Jacob leapt into the genealogy of God's people with quite a splash. As perhaps the least sympathetic of the patriarchs, he certainly makes us as readers scratch our heads. *Who is this guy?*

The answer, unfortunately, is that Jacob is us. At some point in life, we've all lied, manipulated, bargained with God and been unkind. Sometimes we are harshest toward the Bible characters who resemble us the most.

The good news is: God works with Jacobs. He protected Jacob, guided him and blessed him. And if God was good to Jacob, He will be good to us. Jacob had some pretty tough lessons to learn during his time with Laban's family, and we see that God did not shield him from learning some of those lessons the hard way, as he ended up on the receiving end of deception. But those lessons didn't happen because God left Jacob. They happened because *God was with him* (Genesis 28:15; Genesis 31:3).

Sometimes we experience the hard consequences of our sins. Even then, God is with us, protecting, guiding and blessing us as He invites us to seek a fresh start with Him. It's who He is.

Lord, thank You for *being with us* as we change and grow. Thank You for *forgiving* our wrongs and for granting us the *grace* to make things right with people we may have hurt. We are so glad You *never leave us* even when we have messed up. May we learn to anticipate Your *kindness*, and may we trust that Your *goodness* abounds. In Jesus' name, *amen*.

NOTES

NOTES

WEEK
Six

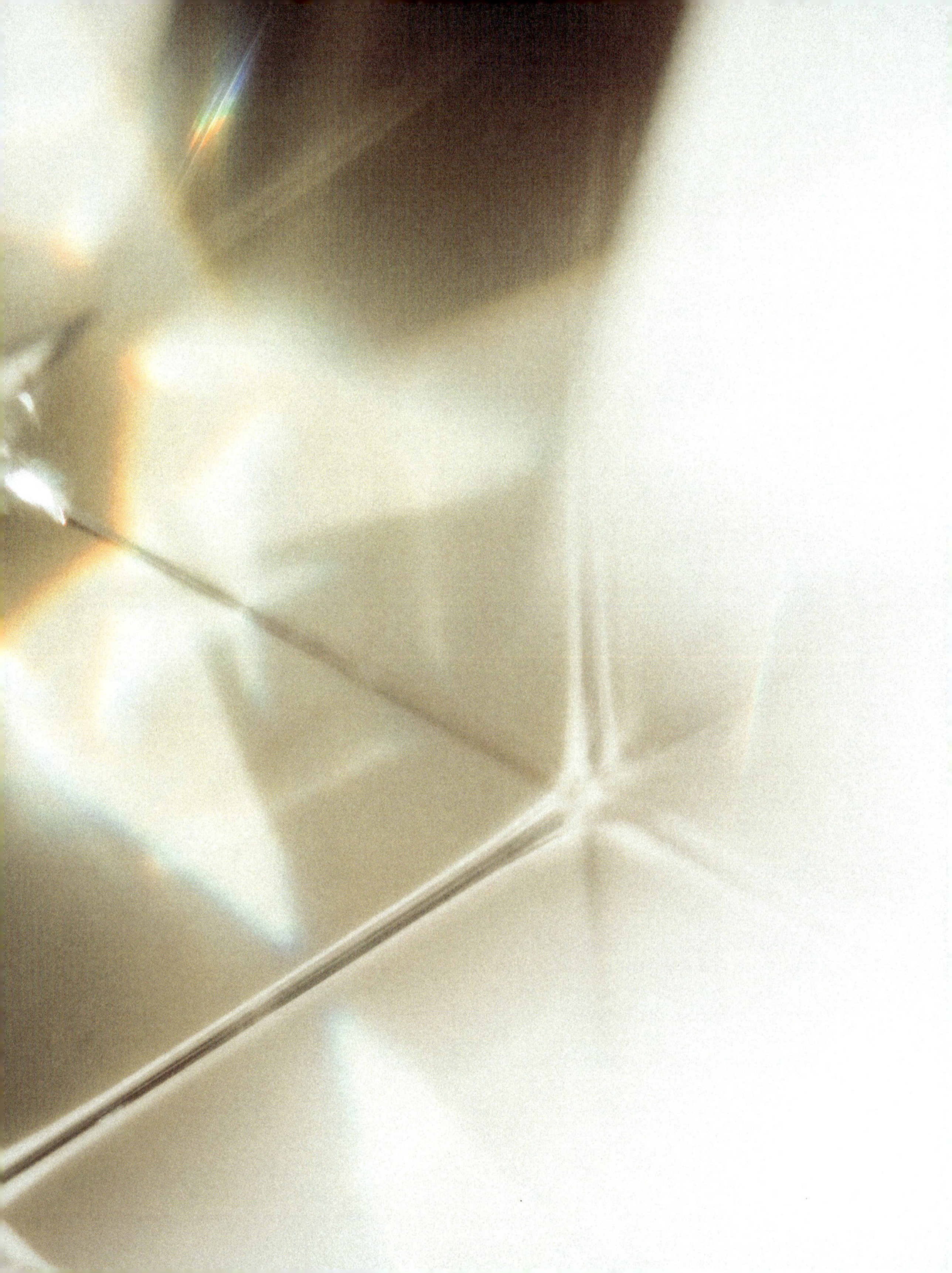

Day 26 - GENESIS **32-33**
Jacob met with Esau and wrestled with God.

On his way back home, Jacob anticipated meeting his brother Esau and sent a message letting Esau know he and his family were coming. The reply terrified Jacob: Esau was coming with 400 men.
- Before we continue, let's recall how Esau felt last time Jacob saw him. Reread Genesis 27:41-42. Based on these verses, how do you think you would have reacted to Esau's 400-man "greeting party" in Genesis 32 if you were Jacob?

Quickly Jacob went on defense, splitting his family and camp into two in case Esau wanted to kill them, so that at least half would survive (Genesis 32:7-8). In reality, Genesis 33:12 clarifies that Esau was coming to escort them into the land, but Jacob prepared for the worst.

Then Jacob prayed his first prayer recorded in Scripture.
- In Genesis 32:9-12, what did Jacob say about himself and how he felt? What did he ask God to do? What did he remind God?

Next, Jacob began to strategically send messages and gifts to appease Esau and likely to slow down his caravan (Genesis 32:13-21). After his time with Laban, Jacob had now been on the receiving end of 20 years of deception. He knew how it felt to be victimized like Esau, and he knew he deserved Esau's rage. The coming confrontation was about more than birthrights and blessings; Jacob was struggling with his own character. Jacob was at the end of himself, and the consequences were coming at him and his family.

Facing our own failures and sins can be terrifying. Even when we're sitting in our living room alone, maybe we feel Jacob's fear of exposure – just like Adam and Eve hiding in shame when God caught them in sin (Genesis 3:8-10). Yet as we will see, the same God who called out to Adam and Eve was the One who met Jacob. And He meets us.
- In Genesis 32:24-29, "*a man*" came to Jacob and wrestled with him. What clues in the passage tell you this was more than just a regular man?

- Write out the order of events in these verses, paying attention to the names requested and given:

Jacob and the man (presumably a manifestation of God Himself), wrestled all night – and God chose not to overpower Jacob. Since God is all-powerful (Psalm 89:8-13), we know He could have easily defeated Jacob right away. God also could have **started** by injuring Jacob's hip, but instead He chose to wrestle the entire night through and **then** *"touched his hip socket"* (Genesis 32:25).

Bible scholar J.I. Packer notes:

> "There was no particle of self-reliance left in Jacob by the time God had finished with him. The nature of Jacob's prevailing with God (32:28) was simply that he had held on to God while God weakened him and wrought in him the spirit of submission and self-distrust; that he had desired God's blessing so much that he clung to God through all this painful humbling, till he came low enough for God to raise him up by speaking peace to him and assuring him that he need not fear about Esau anymore."[1]

In Genesis 32:27, when the all-knowing God asked Jacob to tell his name, He wasn't asking for information; He was asking Jacob to be vulnerable. Jacob had to say, "I am *Jacob*," which meant "I am *Deceiver*." He was confessing how he had sinned against Esau.[2]

To receive God's blessing, Jacob had to declare his sin to God and wait for His response. Jacob could not deceive God as he had deceived Esau and his father. Jacob had to be fully himself with God.

- Read Hosea 12:3-4. What else did Jacob do while wrestling with God? ("*He _____ and sought his favor.*") How does this emphasize his vulnerability?

- God's response to Jacob was to raise him back up. What did God say to Jacob when He renamed him in Genesis 32:28?

His name changed from "Jacob" (meaning "deceiver") to "Israel" (meaning "he strives with God" or "God strives"). In receiving this new name, Jacob accepted God's new direction for his life. In the past, he had used deception and self-reliance to receive a blessing; now he would concede to God's direction. This is how Jacob would become Israel.

Jacob was unruly and would continue in some of his sinful ways … yet God still blessed him, covenanted with him, and used him in His salvation plan.
- Can you think of any Bible characters who were perfect? List them below:

There's only one name on this list: Jesus. And this is good news for us! All of us have sin struggles, but we can praise God for His goodness and mercy to redeem sinners. He takes away our shame and helps us practice goodness and represent Him.

Remember this, friend: Even if we feel like our failures disqualify us from being in God's family, they don't. We can approach Him with confidence, knowing He is good and sits on a throne of grace (Hebrews 4:16).

Day 27 - GENESIS 34

Dinah was assaulted, and her brothers retaliated brutally.

Editor's Note: *This lesson contains sensitive material. To those who have experienced sexual trauma or are triggered by reading texts that discuss sexual trauma, please proceed carefully.*

After the relatively hopeful story of Jacob's exit from Haran, his encounter with God, and his entrance back home, today's Bible story can feel like a gut punch. A terrible crime, silence from those in power, deception and violence all happened in rapid succession. What was going on?

Dinah, Jacob and Leah's daughter, survived an evil violation at the hands of a man named Shechem (Genesis 34:1-2). The Bible cannot be accused of whitewashing the sins of its characters. Even the forefathers of our faith struggled with the temptations of sin, and they often failed. Stories like these are in the Bible because they are tragically part of real life. Held up to the light, they are almost too difficult to bear — but God will not hide His face from our pain.

God saw, and the Bible records, these details about Dinah's suffering:
- Dinah wasn't doing anything wrong by traveling to the city (Genesis 34:1). Shechem *"seized her"* in an act of **his** wrongdoing (v. 2).
- Jacob was silent instead of speaking on behalf of his daughter (v. 5), but he defended his own reputation (v. 30).
- Dinah's brothers expressed concern for her, but on some level, this was likely based on wrongly viewing her as damaged property.[1] They pursued revenge to defend their family honor (vv. 7, 27, 31).
- The brothers dealt *"deceitfully"* with Shechem and Hamor (following in their father, Jacob's, patterns) (v. 13).
- Simeon and Levi committed murder, and the rest of the brothers plundered mercilessly (vv. 25-29; see also Genesis 49:5).

Genesis 34 is a story of disaster. The people in Dinah's life failed her. Her family's response to her assault was to brutally seek revenge and protect their honor.
- How does it feel to know that God includes stories like this one, with unhappy endings, in the Bible? Why might it be valuable to sit with hard parts of Scripture in light of our own hard experiences?

Over 2,000 years later, God in the flesh walked into Shechem (renamed Sychar).[2] Jesus sat by a well and encountered a woman there (John 4:4-42). He treated her with dignity. He mentioned the ex-husbands she had – but not to heap shame on her. He showed gentleness and compassion, acknowledging that her life had been difficult and that He knew all the details.

Jesus saw, and the Bible records, these details about the woman at the well:
- He knew her past and present. She was not just *a woman* to Him (John 4:18-19; John 4:39).
- He listened to her voice. He engaged with her as a person, not as property (John 4:7-26).
- He recognized her longing for God's Truth and gave it to her (John 4:22-26).
- He was concerned about her, not His social reputation (John 4:9; John 4:27).

Jesus could have delivered His message about worshipping God *"in spirit and truth"* (John 4:24) to anyone when He came to a well in ancient Shechem. He chose to speak with this woman and to make her an evangelist to her town (John 4:39-41).
- Are there places with painful significance in your life? Places you don't like to think about or drive by? What would it look like to imagine spiritually meeting with Jesus in one of those very spots? What words of kindness would you find from Him there?

Jesus did what Jacob should have done. Jacob should have sat with Dinah in her pain. He should have listened to her. He should have told her she was valuable, made in the image of God. He should have reflected God's character of justice and righteousness in his response to her rape. Silence and violence were not the right answers.[3,4,5]
- When you face injustice, are you more tempted to be silent or angry and quick to retaliate? Ask God to give you wisdom about what it looks like to represent Him in such situations.

Even though Jacob had interacted with God, and was perhaps even still limping from the exchange (Genesis 32:25), he and his sons were still struggling with their character flaws. Jacob was still Jacob-ing, living as if his name wasn't changed, which is also a cautionary tale for us.

But God didn't leave Jacob even when he fell back into his old ways. And today we, too, can thank God for His mercy in our (sometimes messy) growth.

- What sinful habits or tendencies of the past do you find yourself returning to even as you seek to follow God? Remembering that shame is from the enemy, and proceeding through the lens of God's love and forgiveness, ask God to reveal any lie(s) that persuade you to act based on old sin habits. As you confess to Him, embrace God's forgiveness, knowing you can walk forward in integrity in His favor.

Day 28 - GENESIS **35-36**

Jacob followed through on his promise to God at El-bethel.

In the opening verse of today's passage, God reminded Jacob of the vow he had made more than 20 years before (Genesis 35:1).
- Turn back to Genesis 28:19-22, and/or look back to Day 23 in your study guide. What had Jacob vowed to do? What had he required of God? Where did this take place?

God indeed protected and provided for Jacob and brought him home. Jacob now fulfilled his part of the vow by purifying his family, burying all their foreign gods, and building an altar named El-bethel (in Hebrew, *beth-el* means "house of God"). We aren't told if Jacob tithed (giving God 10% of his wealth) like he promised, but God's response in Genesis 35:9-14 seems to indicate Jacob had satisfied the vow.[1]

God responded by reaffirming Jacob's name change and His covenant with Jacob's father and grandfather. Even though it took over 20 years for unruly Jacob to make it back to this place of promise, Jacob recognized God's faithfulness and kept his own vow.

God's patience is long, and He leans toward mercy.

Next, as they left Bethel and were traveling, we find out Rachel was carrying a child. She died while giving birth to her and Jacob's last son, Benjamin (Genesis 35:16-19).
- After reading about where Rachel was buried, what troubling information do we learn about Reuben, Jacob's eldest son, in Genesis 35:22? How did Jacob respond (or not respond)?

A "*concubine*" (v. 22) in the ANE was similar to a wife but had a lower status in polygamous family arrangements. (Though let's recall that God does not approve of polygamy — and this verse is one example of dysfunction it caused among His people.) Reuben was making a political move by sleeping with his father's concubine, attempting to corral power for himself as a leader before Jacob died.[2] Jacob's apparent silence here was much like his response when Dinah was raped; however, Reuben's move later backfired.

- Looking ahead, what did Jacob say to Reuben in Genesis 49:3-4 when handing out blessings to his sons? What might we learn from this about the long-term effects of unwise choices, even if they seem to have no immediate repercussions?

After Jacob and Esau buried their father, Isaac, Genesis 36 lists Esau's lineage. Esau had five sons, and his descendants became the nation of Edom, as the Lord had told Rebekah (Genesis 25:23). In a story similar to that of Abraham and Lot (Genesis 13:6), Esau left Canaan for *"the hill country"* because the land couldn't support both his and Jacob's families (Genesis 36:6-8).

Esau's family would not carry God's covenant, but God did not forget or ignore their history.
- Reread Genesis 22:18, and note how many nations God said He would bless through His redemption plan.

- Next, read Revelation 7:9. Which nations will be at the throne of heaven? In Matthew 28:18-20, how does Jesus say this will happen?

God chose one family — Abraham, Isaac, Jacob and their descendants — to carry His covenant in the Old Testament. However, inclusion into the covenant would be open to *everyone*; whoever was willing to place their faith in the one true God would be invited to participate in His covenant plan alongside Abraham's extended family (see Hebrews 11).

God carries His plans from beginning to end. He is the first and the last, and His character never changes (Revelation 22:13).

Day 29 – GENESIS 37

Joseph's story began with his dreams and coat of many colors.

Genesis 37:1-2 introduces the last "*generations of*" section in Genesis. Scholars sometimes refer to Genesis 37-50 as the "Joseph Novella" since Joseph is the main character. Right off, in Genesis 37:3, we learn Joseph was Jacob's favorite son. The partiality of Jacob's parents (Genesis 25:28) apparently followed Jacob into his marriage and parenting … and the painful effects of this favoritism would also follow him.

- According to Genesis 37:2, why were Joseph's brothers from Bilhah and Zilpah not fond of him? In verses 4-5, why didn't his brothers from Leah like him? (As a note, remember that Joseph's mom was Rachel, and Benjamin was his only brother who shared the same mom.)

- In Genesis 37:7-11, Joseph had two dreams. How did his brothers relate to Joseph in his dreams? How did they feel about Joseph telling them the dreams?

When his brothers saw Joseph approaching, wearing his special "*robe of many colors*" (vv. 3, 23) that proved their father's preference for him, they plotted to kill him. But in verse 22, Reuben convinced the others to leave Joseph in a pit rather than outright murder him.

- In verses 26-28, whose idea was it to sell Joseph into slavery? Why?

If Joseph were sold, the brothers would profit from the sale *and* there would be one less heir to their father's estate. So they "*sold him to the Ishmaelites for twenty shekels of silver*" (Genesis 37:28). Then they fooled their father, Jacob, into believing Joseph had died.

- How does Genesis 37:31-33 compare to the way Jacob tricked his own father with a disguise years earlier in Genesis 27:18-24? Why might this parallel be significant?

- How did Jacob respond in Genesis 37:34-35 when he thought Joseph was dead?

Jacob, who was silent when his daughter Dinah was assaulted (Genesis 34:5) and when his son Reuben slept with his concubine (Genesis 35:22), had a deep emotional reaction to Joseph's death. He declared he would grieve until he died ("*I shall go down to Sheol*" in Genesis 37:35 was a reference to the grave). Finally: an appropriate response to tragedy.
- Throughout our study, we've had a close-up view of the dysfunction in Jacob's family. Favoritism, hatred and jealousy can wreak havoc on relationships, creating vicious cycles. Have you seen any of these traits in your family? Have you ever found yourself repeating sins or passing them onto the next generation? Let's ask God to free us from any unhealthy cycles so His love, forgiveness and freedom are the legacy we leave behind.

As his father wept, Joseph was sold to a man named Potiphar, "*an officer of Pharaoh, the captain of the guard,*" in Egypt (Genesis 37:36). Would God turn even this into good?

A sneak peek ahead to Genesis 50:20 assures us: He always does.

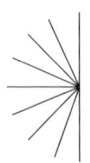

Day 30 - GENESIS 38

Judah was concerned for his property and land, and his family line continued through Tamar.

After Joseph was sold into slavery, his family's life continued in Canaan. Today's scriptures focus on one of Jacob's other sons, Judah, who married and had three sons.

Judah's oldest son, Er, was evil. He married a woman named Tamar, but Genesis 38:7 says the Lord took his life in an act of justice. After Er's death, Judah told his second-born son, Onan, to have a child with Tamar according to ANE customs and laws of the time (Deuteronomy 25:5-6). Onan and Tamar's son would be considered Er's heir and would inherit the double-portion birthright due to the firstborn.
- What was Onan's concern? What did he do in Genesis 38:9?

If Onan could avoid having a child with Tamar, then *he and his children* would inherit the double portion due to Er's family. Out of selfishness, Onan avoided impregnating Tamar, and God punished Onan the same way He did Er (Genesis 38:10).

Sometimes when we read God's judgments in Scripture, they can feel harsh, but Genesis has repeatedly told us of God's mercy and righteousness. God has earned our trust, and we know He handled Judah's sons with long patience and perfect justice.

Failing to perceive God's judgment of his wicked sons, Judah superstitiously regarded Tamar as a wife who brought misfortune. Because Judah was not about to risk the life of his third son, Shelah, by giving him as a husband to Tamar (v. 11), her future was bleak. It seemed she was destined to be stuck in a very hard socioeconomic situation for a woman in the ANE: a childless widow twice over.
- What did she do in Genesis 38:13-19 when she heard Judah was coming into town? What did she ask Judah to give her?

The signet, cord and staff were akin to a modern-day driver's license, a form of ID.[1] When Judah realized they were gone, as was Tamar, he dropped the matter for fear he would look foolish.
- In verse 24, what did Judah say should happen to Tamar when he found out she was pregnant? How was it ironic for Judah to condemn her "*immorality*"?

When Tamar pulled out Judah's identification, he was instantly convicted of his wrongdoing. We may think of prostitution as the most obvious "headline" sin in this story, but Judah also emphasized that he had not fulfilled his obligation to provide for Tamar by marrying her to his son Shelah (v. 26). Cheating a widow was a particularly grievous injustice.

- Tamar herself wasn't perfect; she made broken choices in broken circumstances. Still, what did Judah say about her in verse 26?

In this story filled with brokenness, we still find God's values. He didn't approve of Er's evil or Onan's selfishness, especially at a high cost to others. He saw Tamar stuck in her tragic situation and ultimately brought redemption. In fact, she, a Canaanite woman, is the first person who was called "*righteous*" (v. 26) among the family of Abraham.

- Tamar and Judah had twin sons, Perez and Zerah (Genesis 38:29-30). Flip over to Ruth 4:18-22 to see who was in Perez's family tree (specifically, the final name in verse 22).

- Now look up Matthew 1:3-16. Who came from this family?

There are five women specifically mentioned in Jesus' lineage: Tamar, Rahab, Ruth, Bathsheba (the wife of Uriah), and Mary. They had a variety of backgrounds and heritages but all were ultimately known for their faithfulness and courage. Maybe we'd expect to see Sarah, Rebekah or Leah's names, and they, too, were an important part of the story, but God is drawing our attention to this: He delights to bless us in the places we least see it coming, and His storyline is long.

WEEK SIX
Reflection

This week, we saw that especially after Jacob was deceived at Laban's home, he dreaded meeting Esau, a victim of Jacob's own deception. The patriarch's new life experiences gave him insight into the depth of his sin against Esau.

But before he met Esau, Jacob met God. The same God who had kept him safe and blessed him then wrestled with him through the night. Jacob came to the end of himself, and he left the fight with a new limp … and a new name.

Many of us have experienced a dark night of the soul when we've exhausted our reserves and it feels like we lack the spiritual, emotional and physical resources to continue. We know our best efforts aren't enough to outrun the consequences of our poor decisions.

It's just us and Jesus.

Yet He is not shocked that we've been tossed around by the world. In fact, as He did with the woman at the well, He knows exactly what we need.

Maybe we need Him simply to sit and stay with us.

Or maybe we need Him to grab us tight and let us wrestle until we can't fight Him anymore.

Or maybe we need Him to gently remind us that He has been faithful, even when we've depended on our resources instead of Him.

Or maybe we need Him to do for us what He did for Judah, and what He did for Adam and Eve: clothe our shame with His mercy, recognizing our frailty and providing loving care.

Yes, dark nights of the soul are dark because they are intensely vulnerable. But God is safe there. His presence makes us humble, but He never cruelly humiliates us. When we go to those places where we don't want to go, we will find the company of a good God. All that we are not meets all that He is.

Joseph found himself in such a place at the bottom of a pit in Genesis 37. The family members he thought were safe actually did not like him and did not mind harming him. There he sat at the bottom of the well, and then he was sold, carted off like property for someone else to own. We can imagine he felt helpless, ashamed and enraged. Yet as we will see, a good God still met him there.

To prevail at the end of a dark night is not always to wake up happy and new. To prevail is to walk in humility with a good God. It was true for Israel, and it's true for us.

Lord, thank You for *meeting us* in the dark places. Thank You for *being with us* even when we can't see You clearly. Help us to align ourselves daily with Your character, knowing that with You, we have every *good* thing. May we see clearly how You *love* us and *lead* us. In Jesus' name, *amen*.

NOTES

NOTES

WEEK
Seven

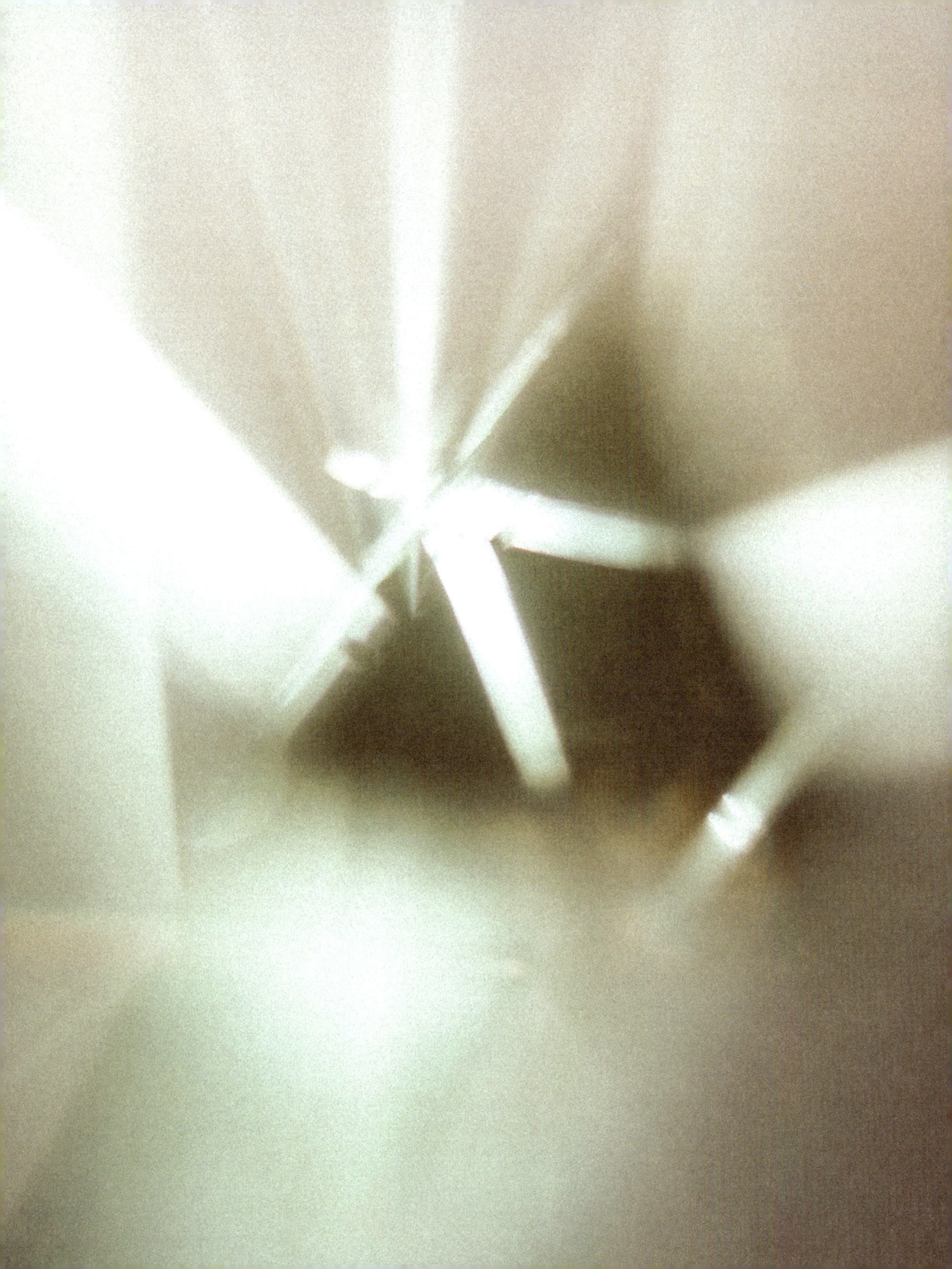

Day 31 - GENESIS 39
Joseph faced challenges in Potiphar's house.

The scene changes as we go from Judah's story in Genesis 38 to Genesis 39, which draws our attention to Joseph's life in Egypt. After his brothers sold him into slavery, Joseph found himself in a prosperous Egyptian household. Of the possibilities available to Joseph as an enslaved worker or servant in the ANE, this was much preferable to outdoor labor.

- The man Joseph worked for in Egypt was named Potiphar. What was Potiphar's title, according to Genesis 39:1? What were Joseph's assignments from Potiphar in verses 4-6a?

The Lord was with Joseph, and he was successful. From small to great responsibilities, Joseph did well. He was blessed, and Potiphar could tell "*the Lord was with him*" (v. 3).

- But in verse 7, Potiphar's wife pursued Joseph with inappropriate and unacceptable sexual advances. What did Joseph say in response in verses 8-9?

Perhaps Joseph was tempted to sleep with Potiphar's wife, but we aren't told (as we are explicitly told about the attractions of other characters in Genesis 24:67, Genesis 29:18 or Genesis 34:3). Genesis 39:10 does tell us Potiphar's wife repeatedly propositioned Joseph "*day after day*" — despite him repeatedly telling her no. However Joseph felt, he responded by appealing to his relationship with Potiphar and, most importantly, with God. He did not want to put either relationship in jeopardy.

- Joseph told Potiphar's wife that if he lay with her, he would be committing a "*great wickedness and sin against God*" (Genesis 39:9). How do you react when someone tries to lead you away from godly convictions? What helps you stay true to godliness in your actions and character?

Keeping the long-term ramifications in mind when making decisions can be hard. If we think about it like managing a bank account, some choices will be more costly than others. And by making purchases without looking at the price tag, we can go broke rather quickly. Joseph understood that sleeping with Potiphar's wife would be very expensive indeed.

One day Potiphar's wife "*caught him by his garment, saying, 'Lie with me.' But he ... fled and got out of the house*" (Genesis 39:12). She then lied about Joseph to the other servants and to Potiphar. Ironically, Joseph's garment was the false "evidence" she used to misrepresent him to Potiphar, much as Joseph's brothers had used his many-colored coat to lie about him to his father in Genesis 37:31-33.

Potiphar was angry. He could have demanded the death penalty for Joseph according to ANE laws.[1] But he instead sent Joseph to jail "*where the king's prisoners were confined*" (Genesis 39:20). As much as this was tragic and very difficult for Joseph, it spared his life and set him up for later interaction with Pharaoh.

Joseph paid a high price when he fled from Potiphar's wife, but it was still less expensive than his other option: sin (Romans 6:23). While he was in jail, Joseph had a clear conscience and a right relationship with God (Genesis 39:21-23). And throughout the rest of this week's study, we'll see that though evil people planned evil against Joseph, his good God would transform it into goodness.
- When have you had an experience where you did the right thing and remained faithful to God, but you felt like it ended in the wrong result? Ask God to show you how He has blessed and will bless your obedience to Him.

Day 32 - GENESIS **40-41**

Joseph interpreted dreams and had a dramatic rise to power in Egypt.

Yesterday we saw that God was with Joseph even in jail, making him successful in all he did. Joseph even became an overseer of the other prisoners (Genesis 39:22-23)! After some time, the Egyptian king, the Pharaoh, was upset with his cupbearer and baker and sent them to the jail where Joseph was in charge (Genesis 40:2-3). Once there, they had some unusual dreams.

In the ANE, many people thought dreams were revelations from the gods, needing interpretation by trained specialists. These specialists in Egypt were called diviner priests or "*magicians*" (Genesis 41:8; Genesis 41:24).[1] So when the cupbearer and baker had dreams in Genesis 40, they were distraught that no one could interpret them — until they asked Joseph.

- Write what the cupbearer and baker dreamed and what Joseph said was the interpretation (we've completed one part for you as an example).

	DREAM	INTERPRETATION
Cupbearer (Genesis 40:9-15)		• Three branches represented three days. • Pharaoh would lift the cupbearer's head. • The cupbearer would again serve Pharaoh.
Baker (Genesis 40:16-19)		

- According to Joseph, who do "*interpretations belong to*" (Genesis 40:8)? How was this truth different from prevailing ideas in his culture?

Diviner priests consulted "dream books" meant to decode dreams, providing determinations (i.e., a dream about XYZ is bad) or predictions from the so-called gods.[2] But later in the Old Testament, the true God told His people not to practice divination like the pagan cultures around them (Deuteronomy 18:10).
- Specifically, how did God say He would speak to His people in Deuteronomy 18:18? What does God's Word say in Hebrews 1:1-3, and how does this encourage you as you seek to hear from God?

Joseph had been in Egypt for 11 years. After interpreting his fellow prisoners' dreams, he asked the cupbearer to remember him — but instead, he was forgotten (Genesis 40:23).
- Two years later, the Pharaoh had two troubling dreams on the same night. In Genesis 41:8, who did he call the next morning? Were they able to help?

When Pharaoh called Joseph to interpret his dream, Joseph again was careful to credit God with the ability to interpret, not himself (Genesis 41:16).
- Based on Genesis 41:38, did Pharaoh realize God was interpreting the dream? Why might this be important in light of God's promises throughout Genesis to reveal Himself to "*all the families of the earth*" (Genesis 12:3)?

Joseph interpreted Pharaoh's dreams, predicting a famine, then gave advice on how to handle the next 14 years (Genesis 41:25-36). Pharaoh liked the strategy so much he made Joseph second in command.

Becoming the Pharaoh's No. 2 was a long, 13-year journey. First, Joseph was sold into slavery; then he did well, and God blessed him in all he did. Next, he was wrongly imprisoned; then he rose to a supervisor position in the jail and built relationships in the palace. He was forgotten for two years; however, his God-given ability to interpret dreams led to an encounter with the king of Egypt. Now Joseph was blessing the Egyptian people.

Joseph probably had a hard time imagining how God could bless him when he was sold into slavery, thrown into jail or forgotten in a cell. But not only did God turn each of those situations around *for* Joseph — He also blessed others *through* Joseph. Joseph was blessed, and he was a blessing, just as God told Abraham his offspring would be (Genesis 12:2-3).

- What areas of your life feel impossibly hard? In prayer, present them to God. Remember that His character is to bless, to show patience and to be merciful. Holding both your very hard reality and God's goodness at the same time, ask for the Holy Spirit's comfort as you wait for His blessing.

BREADMAKING
IN ANCIENT EGYPT

According to historians, wheat and barley were staple agricultural products in Egypt, used to make bread and beer.[1] Bread bakers often worked next to large silos filled with grain to make food for officials and the Egyptian army.[2] The bakeries were divided into two areas, one for flat loaves and the other for bread made in pottery molds.[3] The king's baker in Genesis 40 would have played a part in the supervision of this process.

This image is based on wall paintings found in Egyptian tombs, depicting breadmakers at work.

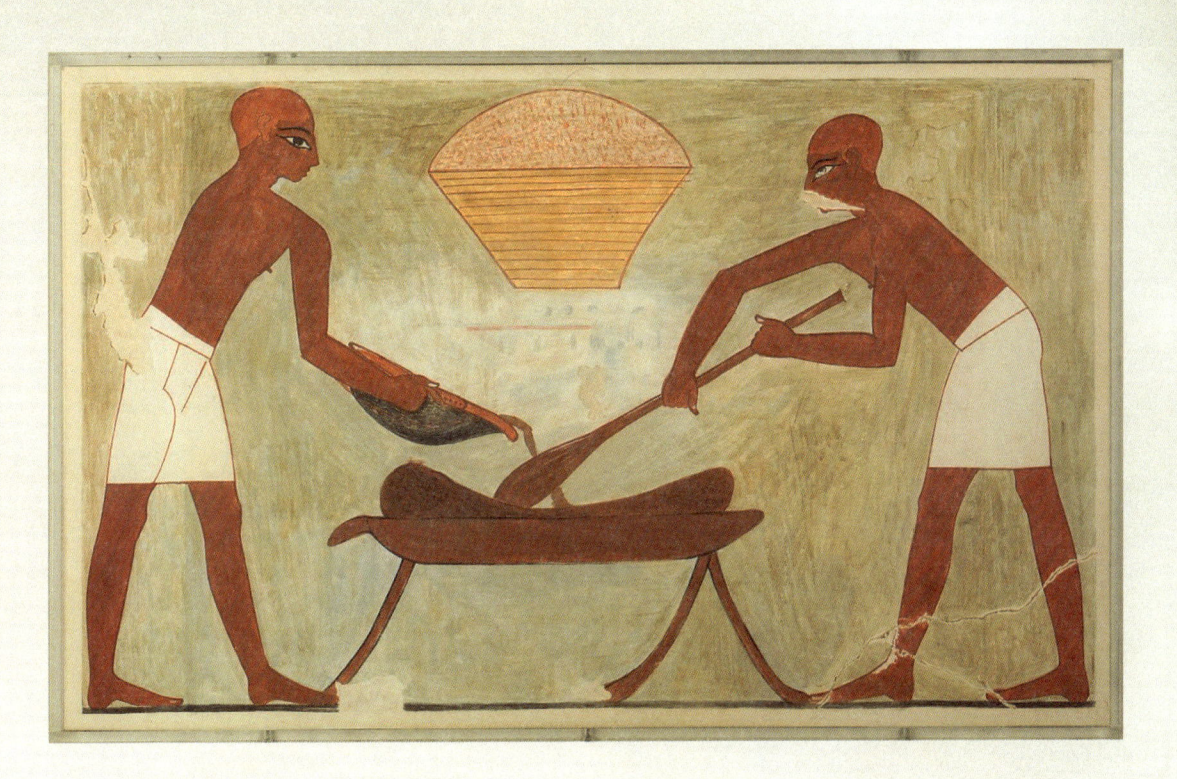

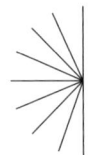

Day 33 - GENESIS **42-45**

Joseph's brothers traveled to Egypt, unaware of Joseph's true identity, leading to a pivotal reunion.

The famine that eventually hit Egypt spread into Canaan and affected Jacob's family. They needed relief, so Jacob sent 10 of his sons to Egypt to buy grain in Genesis 42:1-5. The brothers bowed before Egyptian royalty — including Joseph, whom they didn't recognize after years apart — to ask for food.

They had no idea they were partially fulfilling Joseph's dream that had sent them into a rage more than 20 years earlier (Genesis 37:6-10). But Joseph knew what was happening, and he knew two members of the family were missing: his younger brother (Benjamin) and his father (Jacob).

Over the next three chapters, Joseph put his other brothers through several tests to see if they were still the same jealous and bitter young men they once were.
- In Genesis 42:15-20, after accusing them of being spies, what was the first test Joseph asked them to perform?

- As they were talking among themselves, what did they confess in Genesis 42:21-23? Did they show remorse? Had they changed since Joseph last saw them?

Joseph finally heard them admit that they had ignored his cries from the pit and that they were "*guilty*" of "*sin against*" him (vv. 21-22). What a powerful experience this must have been — it drove Joseph to tears (v. 24).

At the end of Genesis 42, Jacob's sons returned to him with one less son and with more silver than they were supposed to have. They asked to return to Egypt with Benjamin, but Jacob was reluctant to put Benjamin in their hands (Genesis 42:36-37).
- They eventually ran out of food and had to go back. How did Judah convince Jacob to send Benjamin with them in Genesis 43:8-9? How was this a moment of redemption, a fresh start, for Judah after his mess-ups back in Genesis 37-38?

In Genesis 43:16, Joseph saw his brothers coming and put together a feast for them — to their shock. Joseph asked about their father, and when he saw Benjamin, he was filled with compassion and moved to tears again (v. 30). According to verse 33, the brothers then ate together, and Joseph seated them according to age, though no one could have known their birth order outside of their family. Perhaps Joseph was trying to drop a hint about his identity — but they missed it.

- Genesis 43:34 says Benjamin was given a portion five times larger than everyone else's at the feast. How was this overt favoritism similar to how their father had treated Joseph (Genesis 37:3)? Why do you think Joseph wanted to see the brothers' response?

Joseph's final test came when he planted treasure in Benjamin's bag and sent soldiers to arrest him (Genesis 44:1-4). Would the brothers ignore Benjamin's pleas and their father's pain? Was their character unchanged over the last two decades? Would their greed have the final say, or would they show compassion?

- Remember that Judah was the one who sold Joseph in Genesis 37:26-27. How did Judah now respond in Genesis 44:18-34?

At Judah's pleas, "*Joseph could not control himself*" any longer (Genesis 45:1). Boldly revealing his identity to his brothers, he called Jacob "***my** father*" (v. 3, emphasis added). Before, he had asked after *their* father's welfare. But the Hebrew words in verse 3 are familiar in tone and could also be translated as saying something like, "How's Dad?"[1]

As the brothers reunited, Joseph reframed the last 22 years for them. In so many words, he said: All the bad was subject to God's redirection, and all the good was God's elevation and provision.

- The brothers weren't the only ones whose perspectives had changed. Joseph had grown to understand and trust God's ability to turn defeat into victory. How does Genesis 45:5-8 encourage you to trust God today?

Day 34 - GENESIS 46-47:26

Jacob's family moved to Egypt.

When Jacob prepared to leave Canaan, the promised land, to move to Egypt, God visited him in the night in visions. Notably, this was how God visited him every time Jacob left or entered the promised land (Genesis 28:10-22; Genesis 31:11-13; Genesis 32:1; Genesis 32:24-30).
- As a refresher, in Genesis 15:13-16, God had told Abraham (Jacob's grandfather) that his family would take possession of the promised land "*in the fourth generation.*" Why would they have to wait so long?

God wasn't only patient with Israel; He was patient with the Amorites (the peoples who currently lived in the promised land) as well.

What assurance! Yet the prophecy in Genesis 15 also explains one reason Jacob might have been hesitant to go to Egypt, where God said His people would be "*afflicted for four hundred years*" (v. 13).
- Still, what did God tell Jacob in Genesis 46:3-4?

Jacob took his family down to Egypt, and they settled there with everyone intact (Genesis 46:27). God would be with them the entire 400 years, even when they later became slaves, as the book of Exodus records. God always was, and always will be, with His people.

At the end of Genesis 46, we see that after Joseph reunited with his father and extended family, he coached them on how to interact with Pharaoh. Telling Pharaoh they were shepherds made the king more likely to give them the best of the land for their flocks while also ensuring they seemed nonthreatening (since Egyptians considered shepherding an extremely lowly job, according to Genesis 46:34). The meeting went well, and Pharaoh settled Jacob's family in Goshen.

Joseph then continued to lead Egypt through the devastating famine. Let's walk through his steps:
- In Genesis 47:14-16, how did the people first purchase food? And after they were out of money, how did they purchase food?

- After their livestock and money was gone, how did they survive, according to Genesis 47:20-21?

- Who profited from the people and land?

We might say Joseph was helpful in some ways but harsh in others. Acting on insight God Himself had revealed through Pharaoh's dreams, Joseph fed the hungry in Egypt. Eventually it was the Egyptians themselves who offered to serve Pharaoh in exchange for provisions, and Joseph agreed to their proposal. He called for a 20% tribute to Pharaoh, so the Egyptians kept 80% of their crops. They told Joseph, "*You have saved our lives*" (Genesis 47:24-25).

But at the same time, Joseph strategically took advantage of a tough situation by centralizing all the property and wealth for Egypt. As he's one of few upright characters we've encountered in Genesis, it is easy for us to think everything Joseph did was righteous. Later in the Bible, though, God specifically condemns the accumulation of wealth without reprieve. God says He wants the kind of stewardship that protects those in need.
- In Leviticus 25:23-55, God talks about how to treat people who fall on hard times. This includes the brother as well as the stranger. What principles do you notice?

As God's image bearers, we are to follow the principles of mercy laid out in Leviticus 25 and throughout Scripture. Today, this includes principles given to us by Jesus — who reveals the heart behind the Old Testament law (Matthew 18:33; Matthew 5:40-41; Matthew 25:35-45). More than simply being kind to others, God encourages us to go out of our way to seek opportunities for restoration and to bless others in distress.

It's a perspective issue: Do we take advantage of another person's distress for our own betterment, or do we intentionally steward our blessings to *be a blessing to others* so they can thrive?
- Where have you experienced abundance or blessing in your life, and how can you share it with others? Perhaps it's in the form of time, money, supplies or an extra loaf of baked bread. Generosity can take many forms as a wonderful way God shows His creativity.

Day 35 – GENESIS **47:27-50:26**
Jacob blessed his sons.

As we wrap up our study of Genesis with today's final chapters, we see that Israel (Jacob) lived the rest of his days in Egypt, where he and his family "*were fruitful and multiplied greatly*" (Genesis 47:27b).
- Does that verse sound familiar? Look up the verses below, and note who was called to be fruitful and multiply. (For context, you may also need to read a few verses before or after the ones listed.)

    a.   Genesis 1:28:

    b.   Genesis 9:1 and verse 7:

    c.   Genesis 17:2 and verse 6:

    d.   Genesis 26:4 and verse 24:

    e.   Genesis 28:3:

- Why do you think it's important that we see God's fruitfulness command fulfilled here at the end of Genesis?

We learned yesterday that Goshen, where Jacob and his family lived, was the best land in Egypt. No one knows exactly where Goshen was located, but the most probable location was near where the Nile River branches off into the Mediterranean Sea.
- Where else have we seen a garden and rivers in Genesis? (Hint: *"In the beginning ..."*)

- As Genesis shows us the past, the book of Revelation shows us the future: eternal life with God for those who love and follow Jesus. What kind of landscape is described in Revelation 22:1-3? How might this relate to Eden and Goshen?

In a beautiful nod back to Eden and forward to eternity, Genesis reminds us — again — that God is good, that He brings His purposes about no matter what humanity does, and that His plan has a long timeline.

Next in today's passage, Jacob neared the end of his life, and he gave the birthright and his blessing to Joseph and Joseph's two sons. Jacob adopted Joseph's sons, Manasseh and Ephraim, and they took the place of Reuben and Simeon in the Israelite lineage (Genesis 48:5; 1 Chronicles 5:1).[1] Then Jacob continued to give the rest of blessings. These expressed Jacob's expectations for what would happen to his sons after he died.

Here are some highlights:

+ Reuben and his descendants would lose the rights of the firstborn because Reuben slept with Bilhah (Genesis 49:3-4).
+ Simeon and Levi's descendants would be dispersed in the land (Genesis 49:5-7; Joshua 19:1-9) because of these brothers' murderous revenge against Shechem back in Genesis 34. Levi's family would become priests, scattered in towns with pastureland throughout Israel (Joshua 21:3).
+ Judah would be the leader of Israel, even though Joseph received the double-portion birthright.[2] The images and colors in Genesis 49:8-12 indicated leadership, triumph and abundance for Judah.[3]
+ Joseph's descendants would be marked by Jacob's affection and pride toward Joseph (Genesis 49:22-26).

The remainder of the sons received blessings that were callbacks to their births, intertwining the meanings of their names with their futures. Some of these blessings remain elusive to scholars today, or in some cases, it seems Jacob's desires did not happen (for instance, Zebulun seemingly never had territory near a seaside, as Jacob hoped in Genesis 49:13). This aligns with our understanding of fatherly blessings in Scripture as being more like prayer requests than precise prophecies of the future.

At the end of Genesis 49, Jacob died, and his sons were again worried about Joseph exacting revenge on them. They sent a sideways apology in Genesis 50:16-17, admitting their guilt directly to Joseph for the first time.

- How did Joseph respond to their apology in Genesis 50:20? In what ways is this a fitting conclusion for the book of Genesis, after all the human mistakes and messes we've seen God weave into His redemptive plans?

Joseph took the long view of God's plans. He remained committed to forgiveness, leaving the sins of his brothers in God's hands, and did not seek revenge.

So Genesis ends with Israel unified. The God who created the world in Genesis 1 brought about His purposes in it, even after Adam and Eve left the garden. The restoration plan was still in place and ready for the next chapter in God's story.

GENEALOGY OF THE
12 TRIBES OF ISRAEL

From Genesis 12 through Genesis 50, we've walked together through the origin story of Israel by following the family line of Abraham. The 12 sons of Israel (numbered below in their birth order) would become the 12 tribes of the nation of Israel.

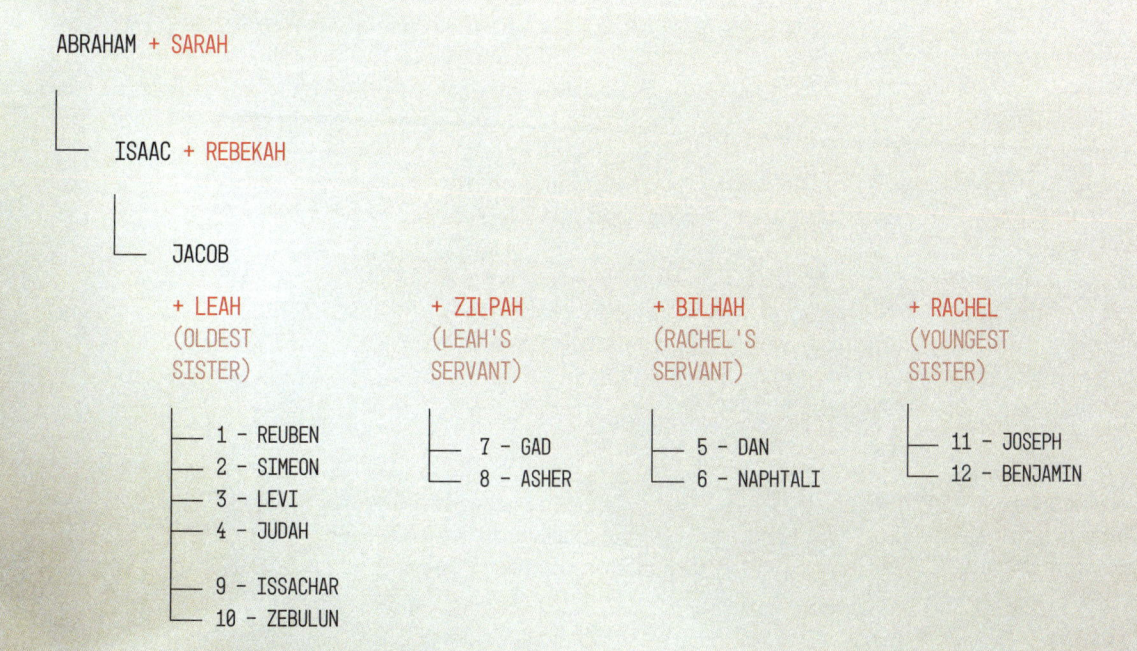

ABRAHAM + SARAH
- ISAAC + REBEKAH
  - JACOB
    - **+ LEAH** (OLDEST SISTER)
      - 1 – REUBEN
      - 2 – SIMEON
      - 3 – LEVI
      - 4 – JUDAH
      - 9 – ISSACHAR
      - 10 – ZEBULUN
    - **+ ZILPAH** (LEAH'S SERVANT)
      - 7 – GAD
      - 8 – ASHER
    - **+ BILHAH** (RACHEL'S SERVANT)
      - 5 – DAN
      - 6 – NAPHTALI
    - **+ RACHEL** (YOUNGEST SISTER)
      - 11 – JOSEPH
      - 12 – BENJAMIN

WEEK **SEVEN**
Reflection

The book of Genesis begins with a good God making good things, who then sat on His throne to reign over His good world. When Adam and Eve wanted to determine what was good and what was evil, they undermined God's authority and order.

Humanity is not meant to take on God's authority. On our own, we aren't good at deciding what is good, as Genesis depicts ... repeatedly. Many times our determination of "good" revolves around what we selfishly think is good for us. Our perspectives get stuck and sidetracked. But God knows what is *actually good* for us. He created flourishing ecosystems where everyone and everything is taken care of by Him, and He called this flourishing world "good." Without understanding God's character and design, we miss God's best for us, settling for our perception of what is good — but God's vision is much bigger and better than we can imagine!

In a beautiful conclusion to the book of Genesis, Joseph declared to his brothers: "*As for you, you meant evil against me, but God meant it for good*" (Genesis 50:20).

So how does God restore His good order when our plans are evil? He sees, He acts, and He blesses. He gives second chances and new beginnings. God wants to help us yield to His good plans. His perspective is not stuck or distracted by evil — He is good and works for good at all times, both in our everyday lives and in the long timeline of human history. And He is still very much on the throne.

We get to walk with this very good God. He wants to bless us and bring about His plans. He invented the concept of thriving, after all! When circumstances in life are overwhelming ... when our best-laid plans slip through our fingers ... when we are facing the consequences of our sins ... Genesis helps us add an "and" to bring perspective on God's character.

My family has dysfunction, **and** *God will help me thrive.*
I lied, **and** *God is safe and will forgive and restore me.*
I can't get ahead right now, **and** *God is with me, working for good.*

It is in this tension where our faith grows. When we hold the truth of His character alongside the truth of our circumstances, we experience the miracle of His presence and witness His goodness. This is the story of Genesis, and this is our story.

Lord, thank You for Your *goodness*. Thank You that You work all things for *good* and that evil will *never* have the final say. We are so thankful for Your long timeline. Please give us *patience* and *perspective* as we sit in the tension of our circumstances and Your character. Please add to our faith. We *love* You and want to *know* You more. In Jesus' name, *amen*.

NOTES

NOTES

END**NOTES**

MAJOR THEMES IN GENESIS

1. Mitchell, Christopher Wright. *The Meaning of BRK "To Bless" in the Old Testament*. Atlanta, GA: The Society of Biblical Literature Dissertation Series, 1987, p. 166.
2. Patty, Tyler J. *Curse and the Power of Blessing: A Linguistic Study of Genesis 1-11*. Deerfield, IL: Moody Bible Institute, 2016, pp. 18-19.
3. Patty, Tyler J. *Curse and the Power of Blessing: A Linguistic Study of Genesis 1-11*. Deerfield, IL: Moody Bible Institute, 2016, p. 146.
4. Patty, Tyler J. *Curse and the Power of Blessing: A Linguistic Study of Genesis 1-11*. Deerfield, IL: Moody Bible Institute, 2016, p. 151.
5. Walton, John. *The NIV Application Commentary: Genesis*. Grand Rapids, MI: Zondervan, 2001, p. 554.
6. Mitchell, Christopher Wright. *The Meaning of BRK "To Bless" in the Old Testament*. Atlanta, GA: The Society of Biblical Literature Dissertation Series, 1987, p. 171.

AUTHOR AND LITERARY FEATURES OF GENESIS

1. Longman, Tremper. *How to Read Genesis*. Downers Grove, IL: InterVarsity Press, 2005, p. 57.
2. Longman, Tremper. *How to Read Genesis*. Downers Grove, IL: InterVarsity Press, 2005, p. 30.
3. Hawk, Daniel L., "Literary/Narrative Criticism," *Dictionary of the Old Testament: Pentateuch*. Downers Grove, IL: InterVarsity Press, 2003, p. 540.
4. Hawk, Daniel L., "Literary/Narrative Criticism," *Dictionary of the Old Testament: Pentateuch*. Downers Grove, IL: InterVarsity Press, 2003, p. 541.
5. Anderson, Bernard W. "From Analysis to Synthesis: The Interpretation of Genesis 1-11," *Journal of Biblical Literature*, vol. 97, no. 1, 1978, p. 38. https://doi.org/10.2307/3265833.

DAY 1

1. Richter, Sandra L. *The Epic of Eden: A Christian Entry into the Old Testament*. Downers Grove, IL: IVP Academic, 2008, p. 102.
2. Smith, Rachel Booth. *Rest Assured: What the Creation Story Was Intended to Reveal About Trusting God*. Chicago, IL: Moody Publishers, 2024, p. 35.

THE IMAGE OF GOD

1. Beckman, Gary. "How Religion Was Done," *A Companion to the Ancient Near East*. Edited by Daniel C. Snell, Malden, MA: Blackwell Pub, 2005, pp. 345-346.
2. Batto, Bernard F. *In the Beginning: Essays on Creation Motifs in the Ancient Near East and the Bible (Siphrut: Literature and Theology of the Hebrew Scriptures)*. Winona Lake, IN: Eisenbrauns, 2013, p. 133.
3. Smith, Rachel Booth. *Rest Assured: What the Creation Story Was Intended to Reveal About Trusting God*. Chicago, IL: Moody Publishers, 2024.

DAY 2

1. "גֶּד," *Hebrew and Aramaic Lexicon of the Old Testament: Study Edition.* Edited by Ludwig Koehler and Walter Baumgartner, Brill Publishers, 2001.
2. Cassuto, U. *A Commentary on the Book of Genesis (Part I): From Adam to Noah.* Translated by Israel Abrahams, Jerusalem: The Magnes Press, The Hebrew University, 1961, p. 134. See also: Walton, John. *The NIV Application Commentary: Genesis.* Grand Rapids, MI: Zondervan, 2001, p. 188.
3. Henry, Matthew. *An Exposition of the Old and New Testament.* Philadelphia: Ed. Barrington & Geo. D. Haswell, 1828, p. 36. https://archive.org/details/expositionofoldn01henr/page/n7/mode/2up.

DAY 4

1. "By the Sweat of Your Brow: Adam, Anat, Athirat and Ashurbanipal," *Ugarit and the Bible: Proceedings of the International Symposium on Ugarit and the Bible.* Edited by George J. Brooke, Adrian Curtis, and John F. Healy, Ugarit-Verlag: Munster, 1994, p. 100.
2. "By the Sweat of Your Brow: Adam, Anat, Athirat and Ashurbanipal," *Ugarit and the Bible: Proceedings of the International Symposium on Ugarit and the Bible.* Edited by George J. Brooke, Adrian Curtis, and John F. Healy, Ugarit-Verlag: Munster, 1994, p. 99.

DAY 6

1. "רבץ," *Hebrew and Aramaic Lexicon of the Old Testament: Study Edition.* Edited by Ludwig Koehler and Walter Baumgartner, Brill Publishers, 2001.
2. Brueggemann, Walter. *Genesis.* Louisville, KY: John Knox Press, 1982, pp. 60-61.

DAY 7

1. Provan, Iain. *Discovering Genesis: Content, Interpretation, Reception.* Grand Rapids, MI: Eerdmans, 2015, p. 101.

DAY 8

1. "קֶשֶׁת," *Hebrew and Aramaic Lexicon of the Old Testament: Study Edition.* Edited by Ludwig Koehler and Walter Baumgartner, Brill Publishers, 2001.
2. Hamilton, Victor P. *The Book of Genesis: Chapters 1-17.* Grand Rapids, MI: Eerdmans, 1990, p. 238.

LITERARY CHIASM OF THE STORY OF NOAH

1. Anderson, Bernard W. "From Analysis to Synthesis: The Interpretation of Genesis 1-11," *Journal of Biblical Literature,* vol. 97, no. 1, 1978, p. 38. https://doi.org/10.2307/3265833.

DAY 9

1. Goldingay, John. *Genesis.* Grand Rapids, MI: Baker Academic, 2020, pp. 166-170.
2. Wenham, Gordon. *Rethinking Genesis 1-11: Gateway to the Bible.* Wipf and Stock Publishers, 2015, p. 64.
3. Wenham, Gordon. *Rethinking Genesis 1-11: Gateway to the Bible.* Wipf and Stock Publishers, 2015, p. 65.

DAY 10

1. Brueggemann, Walter. *Genesis*. Louisville, KY: John Knox Press, 1982, p. 105.

DAY 12

1. Murnane, William J. *The Road to Kadesh: A Historical Interpretation of the Battle Reliefs of King Seti I at Karnak*. Chicago, IL: Oriental Institute of Chicago, 1985, pp. 95-97.

DAY 13

1. Provan, Iain. *Seriously Dangerous Religion: What the Old Testament Really Says and Why It Matters*. Waco, TX: Baylor University Press, 2014, p. 177.

DAY 15

1. Walton, John. *The NIV Application Commentary: Genesis*. Grand Rapids, MI: Zondervan, 2001, p. 451.

WHAT DOES THE ABRAHAMIC COVENANT MEAN FOR US TODAY?

1. Cassuto, U. *A Commentary on the Book of Genesis (Part I): From Adam to Noah*. Translated by Israel Abrahams, Jerusalem: The Magnes Press, The Hebrew University, 1961, p. 291.

DAY 16

1. Walton, John. *The NIV Application Commentary: Genesis*. Grand Rapids, MI: Zondervan, 2001, p. 482.
2. Wenham, Gordon. *World Biblical Commentary: Genesis 16-50*. Dallas, TX: Word Books, 1994, p. 55.

DAY 19

1. Walton, John. *The NIV Application Commentary: Genesis*. Grand Rapids, MI: Zondervan, 2001, p. 510.

DAY 21

1. Albertz, Rainer and Rüdiger Schmitt. *Family and Household Religion in Ancient and the Levant*. Eisenbrauns, 2012, p. 246.
2. Walton, John. *The NIV Application Commentary: Genesis*. Grand Rapids, MI: Zondervan, 2001, p. 549.

DAY 23

1. Dalley, Stephanie. "Nergal and Ereshkigal," *The Context of Scripture*. Edited by William W. Hallo and K. Lawson Younger, Brill Publishers, 2003.
2. Walton, John. *The NIV Application Commentary: Genesis*. Grand Rapids, MI: Zondervan, 2001, p. 570.

DAY 24

1. Wenham, Gordon. *World Biblical Commentary: Genesis 16-50*. Dallas, TX: Word Books, 1994, p. 235.
2. Finkelstein, Jacob Joel. "An Old Babylonian Herding Contract and Genesis," *Journal of the American Oriental Society*, vol. 88, no. 1, Jan-March 1968, p. 35.

DAY 25

1. Flynn, Shawn W. "The Teraphim in Light of Mesopotamian and Egyptian Evidence," *The Catholic Bible Quarterly*, vol. 74, no. 4, October 2012, p. 711.
2. Steinmann, Andrew E. *Genesis: An Introduction and Commentary (Tyndale Old Testament Commentaries)*. Edited by David G. Firth and Tremper Longman, InterVarsity Press, 2019, p. 287.

DAY 26
1. Packer, J.I. *Knowing God*. Downers Grove, IL: InterVarsity Press, 1973, p. 96.
2. Wenham, Gordon. *World Biblical Commentary: Genesis 16-50*. Dallas, TX: Word Books, 1994, p. 296.

DAY 27
1. Walton, John. *The NIV Application Commentary: Genesis*. Grand Rapids, MI: Zondervan, 2001, p. 629.
2. Keener, Craig. *The Gospel of John: A Commentary*, vol 1. Peabody, MA: Holbrook Publishers, 2003, p. 590.
3. Armstrong, Kat. "Shechem Parts 1-5," *Holy Curiosity with Kat Armstrong*. Podcast, season 1, episodes 1-5, March/April 2024. https://podcasts.apple.com/us/podcast/holy-curiosity-with-kat-armstrong/id1726055394.
4. Armstrong, Kat. *The In-Between Place: Where Jesus Changes Your Story*. Thomas Nelson, 2021.
5. Langberg, Diane. *Redeeming Power, Understanding Authority and Abuse in the Church*. Brazos Press, 2020.

DAY 28
1. Wenham, Gordon. *World Biblical Commentary: Genesis 16-50*. Dallas, TX: Word Books, 1994, p. 325.
2. Waltke, Bruce K. *Genesis: A Commentary*. Grand Rapids, MI: HarperCollins Christian Publishing, 2001, p. 478.

DAY 30
1. Walton, John. *The NIV Application Commentary: Genesis*. Grand Rapids, MI: Zondervan, 2001, p. 669.

DAY 31
1. *A History of Ancient Near Eastern Law*, vol. 1. Edited by Raymond Westbrook, Leiden, Netherlands: Brill Publishers, 2003, p. 80.

DAY 32
1. Wenham, Gordon. *World Biblical Commentary: Genesis 16-50*. Dallas, TX: Word Books, 1994, p. 391.
2. *Dreams and Dream Narratives in the Biblical World*. Translated by Jean-Marie Husser with Jill Munro, Sheffield, England: Sheffield Academic Publishing, 1999, pp. 66-67.

BREADMAKING IN ANCIENT EGYPT
1. Kemp, Barry J. *Ancient Egypt: Anatomy of a Civilization*. New York, NY: Routledge, 2006, p. 178.
2. Papazian, Hratch. "The Central Administration of the Resources in the Old Kingdom: Departments, Treasuries, Granaries and Work Centers," *Ancient Egyptian Administration*. Edited by Juan Carlos Moreno Garcia, Leiden, Netherlands: Brill Publishers, 2013, p. 59.
3. Kemp, Barry J. *Ancient Egypt: Anatomy of a Civilization*. New York, NY: Routledge, 2006, p. 172.

DAY 33
1. Walton, John. *The NIV Application Commentary: Genesis*. Grand Rapids, MI: Zondervan, 2001, p. 682.

DAY 35
1. de Hoop, Raymond. *Genesis 49 in its Literary and Historical Context*. Leiden, Netherlands: Brill Publishers, 2021, p. 335.
2. de Hoop, Raymond. *Genesis 49 in its Literary and Historical Context*. Leiden, Netherlands: Brill Publishers, 2021, pp. 346-352.
3. Wenham, Gordon. *World Biblical Commentary: Genesis 16-50*. Dallas, TX: Word Books, 1994, pp. 476-479.

NOTES

NOTES

NOTES

NOTES

NOTES

NOTES

NOTES

NOTES

JOIN OUR NEXT STUDY ...

Here for You: Real Community in a Disconnected World, A Study of the Book of Acts

AVAILABLE FEBRUARY 2025
AT P31BOOKSTORE.COM